Steadman

# Survivors

Jamestown's Critical Reading Program

# Survivors

15 Stories of Courage and Fortitude – with Exercises for Developing Reading Comprehension and Critical Thinking Skills

McGraw Hill Education

Bothell, WA • Chicago, IL • Columbus, OH • New York, NY

**mheonline.com**

 **Education**

Send all inquiries to:
McGraw-Hill Education
130 E. Randolph, Suite 400
Chicago, IL 60601

ISBN: 978-0-07-659071-1
MHID: 0-07-659071-2

Printed in the United States of America.

2 3 4 5 6 7 8 9 QDB 15 14 13 12 11

The McGraw·Hill Companies

# Contents

## Unit One

## Unit Two

## Unit Three

# To the Student

If there is one thing certain in life, it is that nothing is at all certain. Just scan some Internet headlines, and you'll find stories of people who were caught in natural disasters and accidents, or who became lost, stranded, or trapped in the crossfire of war.

How people find a solution for these problems is what the real-life stories in this book are all about. *Survivors* contains true accounts of people who formed a plan, put the plan into action, and then learned that the plan had changed to a desperate, dangerous, and possibly fatal situation. What would you do if your boat sped away, leaving you floating in shark-infested waters? How would you deal with being lost on a mountain, taken hostage in a foreign country, or trapped in a flooded mine? The answer is: You would switch to Plan B. You would figure out how to survive.

What is the formula for survival? The people in these stories might tell you that survival requires more stamina than strength. You also need enough courage to stay calm and to keep an open mind for any possible escape. Some call this formula Survival Mode.

As you read these fascinating stories, try to think as a survivor would and imagine yourself in the middle of the ordeal. Consider the options that might be available to you. Try to predict the risks as well as the opportunities. Ask yourself what you would do if the survivor were you.

*Survivors* is for students who already read fairly well but who want to read faster and to increase their understanding of what they read. If you complete the 15 lessons—reading the articles and completing the exercises—you will surely increase your reading speed and improve your reading comprehension and critical thinking skills. Also, because these exercises include items of the types often found on state and national tests, you will find that learning how to complete them will prepare you for tests you may have to take in the future.

# How to Use This Book

**About the Book.** *Survivors* contains three units, each of which includes five lessons. Each lesson begins with an article about a unique event, person, or group. The article is followed by a group of four reading comprehension exercises and a set of three critical thinking exercises. The reading comprehension exercises will help you understand the article. The critical thinking exercises will help you think about what you have read and how it relates to your own experience.

At the end of each lesson, you will also have the opportunity to give your personal response to some aspect of the article and then to assess how well you understood what you read.

**The Sample Lesson.** Working through the sample lesson, the first lesson in the book, with your class or group will demonstrate how a lesson is organized. The sample lesson explains how to complete the exercises and score your answers. The correct answers for the sample exercises and sample scores are printed in lighter type. In some cases, explanations of the correct answers are given. The explanations will help you understand how to think through these question types.

If you have any questions about how to complete the exercises or score them, this is the time to get the answers.

**Working Through Each Lesson.** Begin each lesson by looking at the photographs and reading the captions. Before you read, predict what you think the article will be about. Then read the article.

Sometimes your teacher may decide to time your reading. Timing helps you keep track of and increase your reading speed. If you have been timed, enter your reading time in the box at the end of the article. Then use the Words-per-Minute Table to find your reading speed, and record your speed on the Reading Speed graph at the end of the unit.

Next, complete the Reading Comprehension and Critical Thinking exercises. The directions for each exercise will tell you how to mark your answers. When you have finished all four Reading Comprehension exercises, use the answer key provided by your teacher to check your work. Follow the directions after each exercise to find your score. Record your Reading Comprehension scores on the graph at the end of each unit. Then check your answers to the Author's Approach, Summarizing and Paraphrasing, and Critical Thinking exercises. Fill in the Critical Thinking chart at the end of each unit with your evaluation of your work and comments about your progress.

At the end of each unit you will also complete a Compare and Contrast chart. The completed chart will help you see what the articles have in common. It will also give you an opportunity to explore what you think and feel about each of these survival stories and the people who became involved in them.

Sample Lesson

# Digging Out from Disaster

Haiti officials inspect the ruins of the National Palace after the earthquake in January 2010.

I f you were to compare earthquakes simply by their power—their rumble and shake—the earthquake that struck Haiti on January 12, 2010, was not unusually severe. It measured 7.0 on the Richter scale. Each year around the world, there are about 20 earthquakes that are as powerful. But if you were to measure an earthquake by its effect on a place, two factors would qualify the earthquake that rocked Haiti as particularly intense. First, it struck the poorest country in the Western Hemisphere. Most people in this Caribbean island nation live in extreme poverty. As a result, many of the homes are made of cheap or defective materials. A large number of them are poorly constructed and lack strong foundations. Second, the earthquake struck in a heavily populated region. Its source was just 10 miles west of Port-au-Prince, which is the capital city and home to 2 million people.

2    Given these factors, the chaos that followed in and around Port-au-Prince was not surprising. Practically all of the basic services, including transportation and communication, ceased to function. Huge piles of debris and concrete clogged city streets, making it nearly impossible for fire and police vehicles to get through. People roamed the streets with flashlights looking for loved ones. Some tried to dig victims out from under the rubble with their bare

hands. Still others looked for food, supplies, or vehicles that might have been spared. "Everybody is just totally, totally freaked out and shaken," said U.S. official Henry Bahn while witnessing the event. He described the sky as "just gray with dust." Whole neighborhoods in Port-au-Prince simply collapsed from the quake or from one of the number of large aftershocks. Even the massive Presidential Palace and the National Assembly building suffered extreme damage.

3   The disaster left hundreds of thousands of Haitians homeless. People camped out in temporary shelters without sufficient food, water, or medical care. Days of blazing tropical heat killed or weakened an already fragile population. Dead bodies were burned or buried in mass graves as soon as possible to reduce the odor and prevent the spread of disease. Haitian officials estimated that 230,000 people died in the earthquake. Outside estimates put the total closer to 100,000. Whatever the actual number, in terms of sheer misery, this disaster is one of the worst in recent human history.

4   When rescue workers from around the world arrived with search dogs, special cameras, and heavy digging tools, they mostly unearthed dead bodies. There were some incredible survival stories, though. Seven days after the earthquake, rescuers discovered 18-day-old Elisabeth Joassaint alive and uninjured. She had been asleep in her crib when the earthquake struck. The house had collapsed around her, but the

infant happened to be in a small pocket of space that was left untouched. Elsewhere, six people were trapped under the collapsed Montana Hotel and survived three days by sharing a single lollipop. An 11-year-old girl spent eight days trapped under her home before neighbors heard her cries and dug her out. The first thing she

asked for was a bowl of corn flakes and milk. Seventeen-year-old Darlene Etienne rejoiced when she was rescued from the ruins of her home after 15 days. She was able to survive by drinking water from a bathtub. However, it was seven-year-old Kiki Joachin who most symbolized the hope of those who searched for survivors.

*A team of 20 rescue workers labored for four hours to rescue Kiki and his sister from a collapsed apartment building in Port-au-Prince.*

5    Kiki had been at home with most of his family when the earthquake struck. He and his sister, 10-year-old Sabrina, had been sitting at the table doing homework. Three of his other siblings were nearby, and his brother David was playing outside of the apartment building. As Kiki's mother, Odinal, later recalled, "I was preparing rice and beans for dinner when the whole six-story block fell flat in seconds."

6    Odinal managed to dig herself out from under the ruins. Then she called out for her children, but heard nothing. She later said, "I could see layers of concrete lying on the spot where Kiki had been doing his homework beside his sister. I was sure they were dead."

7    Odinal and her husband assumed that all of their children except David had died in the earthquake. In fact, when the house collapsed, nine-year-old Yeye and 18-month-old Didine were killed instantly. Kiki and Sabrina, however, managed to duck under the table along with their three-year-old brother Titite. They found themselves trapped in the dark cramped space, alive but unable to move under the mounds of debris. Day after day they remained buried there. Little Titite cried desperately for water. Sabrina later said, "He asked us for water on Wednesday on Thursday and Friday." There was no way Kiki or Sabrina could help him or bring him any water. Sabrina later told reporters, "Titite died right next to me."

8    Nine days after the earthquake, the children's aunt, Denival Orana, returned to the apartment building to see if she could salvage any of the family's belongings. As she later told reporters, "I heard, 'Mama! Help us, Mama! Water!'" She recognized the voice as that of her nephew Kiki. "Then I heard his sister call out as well," she said. Quickly Orana ran for help, summoning a 20-member rescue team that had come to Haiti from the United States. The rescuers worked carefully, taking turns digging and cutting through five layers of crushed concrete. At last, after four hours, they cut a hole through the bottom floor and made an opening big enough for rescue worker Chris Dunic to see Kiki huddled amid the rubble and wreckage. Dunic urged Kiki to move toward him, but Kiki was afraid to leave Sabrina. He shook his head and shrank away. Only when Orana called out to Kiki, reassuring him that it was okay to come forward, did the boy move into Dunic's arms. As Kiki was lifted to safety, he broke into a big grin and stretched out his arms

skyward. That image, which was distributed around the world, provided a moment of joy during the terrible tragedy.

9    Because Sabrina was wedged beneath a metal chair pinned down by piles of broken concrete, it took a little longer to get her out. Soon, though, she, too, was safely out of the rubble. Dr. Dario Gonzalez, who was part of the rescue effort, was amazed by Kiki and Sabrina's survival. "These two kids had some kind of luck," he said. Gonzalez compared the rescue of Kiki and Sabrina to giving birth. "We went into labor for hours, and these two children came out of the earth." ✷

*If you have been timed while reading this article, enter your reading time below. Then turn to the Words-per-Minute Table on page 55 and look up your reading speed (words per minute). Enter your reading speed on the graph on page 56.*

**Reading Time: Sample Lesson**

_____ : _____
*Minutes         Seconds*

## A Finding the Main Idea

One statement below expresses the main idea of the article. One statement is too general, or too broad. The other statement explains only part of the article; it is too narrow. Label the statements using the following key:

**M—Main Idea**    **B—Too Broad**    **N—Too Narrow**

___N___ 1. Haitian officials estimate that 230,000 people died in the earthquake on January 12, 2010, but others estimate that the number killed was closer to 100,000. [This statement is true, but it is *too narrow*. This statement mentions only a few of the details from the article.]

___B___ 2. The fact that earthquakes can be extremely damaging and tragic was proved again by a terrible 2010 earthquake in Haiti. [This statement is true, but it is *too broad*. It does not provide enough information about the earthquake or the days that followed it.]

___M___ 3. The earthquake that struck Haiti on January 12, 2010, caused great suffering because of its strength and location, but along with the tragedy there were stories of strength and survival. [This statement is the *main idea*. It tells you that the article describes the terrible disaster of the earthquake and provides a few examples of good fortune and courage.]

___15___ Score 15 points for a correct M answer.

___10___ Score 5 points for each correct B or N answer.

___25___ **Total Score:** Finding the Main Idea

## B Recalling Facts

How well do you remember the facts in the article? Put an X in the box next to the answer that correctly completes each statement about the article.

1. The January 12, 2010, earthquake was centered near
   ☒ a. Haiti's capital city.
   ☐ b. a small town on Haiti's coast.
   ☐ c. a rural area away from any big city.

2. After the quake, dead bodies were buried quickly to
   ☐ a. hide the number of people who had died.
   ☐ b. follow strict religious rules.
   ☒ c. prevent the spread of disease.

3. Infant Elisabeth Joassaint survived by
   ☐ a. sucking on a lollipop.
   ☒ b. being lucky enough to be in a small space not filled with debris.
   ☐ c. drinking water from a bathtub.

4. Kiki and Sabrina Joachin survived under rubble for
   ☒ a. 9 days.
   ☐ b. 15 days.
   ☐ c. 3 weeks.

5. Of the survivors mentioned in the article, the person who was trapped for the most days before being rescued was
   ☐ a. 10-year-old Sabrina Joachin.
   ☒ b. 17-year-old Darlene Etienne.
   ☐ c. 18-day-old Elisabeth Joassaint.

Score 5 points for each correct answer.

___25___ **Total Score:** Recalling Facts

# C Making Inferences

When you combine your own experiences and information from a text to draw a conclusion that is not directly stated in that text, you are making an inference. Below are five statements that may or may not be inferences based on information in the article. Label the statements using the following key:

**C—Correct Inference**          **F—Faulty Inference**

__C__  1.  The earthquake struck in late afternoon or early evening. [This is a *correct* inference. One survivor had been cooking dinner when it struck.]

__F__  2.  After the earthquake, most Haitians built stronger homes. [This is a *faulty* inference. Haitians who were poor before the quake were probably still unable to afford strong homes.]

__F__  3.  The most dangerous place to be during an earthquake is outdoors. [This is a *faulty* inference. David Joachin was playing outside, and he survived the quake.]

__C__  4.  The survivors under the Montana Hotel got along well with each other. [This is a *correct* inference. They cooperated by sharing a single lollipop for three days.]

__C__  5.  It is impossible to know exactly how many people died in the earthquake in Haiti. [This is a *correct* inference. It is likely that no one knows how many people were buried in the mass graves or burned.]

---

Score 5 points for each correct answer.

__25__  **Total Score**: Making Inferences

---

# D Using Words Precisely

Each numbered sentence below contains an underlined word or phrase from the article. Following the sentence are three definitions. One definition is closest to the meaning of the underlined word. One definition is opposite or nearly opposite. Label those two definitions using the following key. Do not label the remaining definition.

**C—Closest**          **O—Opposite or Nearly Opposite**

1.  Many of the homes are made of cheap or <u>defective</u> materials.
    __O__  a.  free from errors or faults
    ____  b.  expensive
    __C__  c.  poorly made; less than perfect

2.  Huge piles of <u>debris</u> and concrete clogged city streets, making it nearly impossible for fire and police vehicles to get through.
    __C__  a.  remains of something broken or destroyed
    __O__  b.  upright structures, such as buildings
    ____  c.  metal or plastic

3.  People camped out in temporary shelters without <u>sufficient</u> food, water, or medical care.
    ____  a.  pure
    __O__  b.  not enough
    __C__  c.  as much as needed

4.  Days of blazing tropical heat killed or weakened an already <u>fragile</u> population.
    __O__  a.  strong
    ____  b.  unhappy
    __C__  c.  weak

5. Nine days after the earthquake, the children's aunt, Denival Orana, returned to the apartment building to see if she could <u>salvage</u> any of the family's belongings.

   _C_   a. recover, save

   _0_   b. get rid of

   _____   c. locate

---

_15_ Score 3 points for each correct C answer.

_10_ Score 2 points for each correct O answer.

_25_ **Total Score**: Using Words Precisely

---

Enter the four total scores in the spaces below, and add them together to find your Reading Comprehension Score. Then record your score on the graph on page 57.

| Score | Question Type | Sample Lesson |
|---|---|---|
| _25_ | Finding the Main Idea | |
| _25_ | Recalling Facts | |
| _25_ | Making Inferences | |
| _25_ | Using Words Precisely | |
| _100_ | **Reading Comprehension Score** | |

## Author's Approach

Put an X in the box next to the correct answer.

1. The main purpose of the first paragraph is to
   ☐ a. explain the purpose of the Richter Scale.
   ☐ b. summarize the effects of Haiti's earthquake.
   ☒ c. explain why Haiti's earthquake was so damaging.

2. From the statements below, choose the one that you believe the author would agree with.
   ☒ a. An earthquake of this size harmed Haiti more than it might have harmed a richer country.
   ☐ b. The earthquake will not have any long-lasting effects in Haiti.
   ☐ c. Rescuers were surprised to find any survivors.

3. Choose the statement below that best describes the author's opinion in paragraph 3.
   ☐ a. Haitians may have reacted too quickly in burning or burying bodies soon after the quake.
   ☒ b. Haitians will be affected by the 2010 earthquake for many years.
   ☐ c. Haitian officials were more accurate than outsiders were when they estimated the number of deaths.

4. The author probably wrote this article in order to
   ☐ a. prove that humans cannot control nature.
   ☐ b. persuade readers to contribute to Haitian relief funds.
   ☒ c. show that some people can survive the worst disasters.

---

_4_ Number of correct answers

Record your personal assessment of your work on the Critical Thinking Chart on page 58.

**CRITICAL THINKING**

## Summarizing and Paraphrasing

Follow the directions provided for questions 1 and 2. Put an X in the box next to the correct answer for question 3.

1. Complete the following one-sentence summary of the article using the lettered phrases from the phrase bank below. Write the letters on the lines.

> **Phrase Bank:**
> a. the miracle survival of several people days after the quake
> b. a description of Haiti before and right after the earthquake
> c. how rescuers saved Kiki and Sabrina Joachin

The article, "Digging Out from Disaster" begins with __b__, goes on to describe __a__, and ends with __c__.

2. Look for the important ideas and events in paragraphs 5 and 6. Summarize those paragraphs in one or two sentences.

Summaries should include the activities of the family

before the earthquake, the sudden collapse of the building,

and which family members were buried and were not buried

in the collapse.

_____

_____

_____

3. Read the statement about the article below. Then read the paraphrase of that statement. Choose the reason that best tells why the paraphrase does not say the same thing as the statement.

Statement: Three children—Kiki, Sabrina, and Titite Joachin—were trapped below mounds of debris for days after the quake.

Paraphrase: Following the quake, three children—Kiki, Sabrina, and Titite Joachin—spent several days trapped under rubble, but only Kiki and Sabrina survived the ordeal.

☒ a. Paraphrase says too much. [This paraphrase adds the information that Titite did not survive.]

☐ b. Paraphrase doesn't say enough.

☐ c. Paraphrase doesn't agree with the statement.

> __3__ Number of correct answers
>
> Record your personal assessment of your work on the Critical Thinking Chart on page 58.

## Critical Thinking

Follow the directions provided for questions 1, 3, and 4. Put an X in the box next to the correct answer for question 2.

1. For each statement below, write O if it expresses an opinion or write F if it expresses a fact.

__F__ a. The earthquake that struck Haiti in 2010 measured 7.0 on the Richter Scale. [This statement is a *fact*; it can be proved.]

__O__ b. All homes should be built strong enough to withstand an earthquake. [This statement is an *opinion*; it cannot be proved.]

__F__ c. The earthquake destroyed the homes of hundreds of thousands of Haitians. [This statement is a *fact*; it can be proved.]

2. From what the article told about the amount and kind of food that the people trapped under the Montana Hotel ate, you can predict that they

☒ a. could not have survived much longer.

☐ b. could have survived under the debris for many more days.

☐ c. could have eaten other kinds of food if they wanted to.

3. Choose from the letters below to correctly complete the following statement. Write the letters on the lines.

On the positive side, __b__, but on the negative side, __a__.

a. hundreds of thousands of people lost their lives

b. there were a few amazing examples of survival

c. the earthquake occurred on January 12, 2010

4. Choose from the letters below to correctly complete the following statement. Write the letters on the lines.

According to the article, __c__, which caused them to __a__, and the effect was __b__.

a. live in poorly constructed homes

b. most Haitian homes were destroyed by the earthquake

c. most Haitian people live in poverty

---

__4__ Number of correct answers

Record your personal assessment of your work on the Critical Thinking Chart on page 58.

---

## Personal Response

What new question do you have about this topic?

[You may be curious about topics mentioned in this article such as earthquakes, Haiti, or the living conditions of the Haitian people. Record that question here.]

## Self-Assessment

Before reading this article, I already knew

[You may have already heard about the earthquake in Haiti or about other earthquakes. You may know stories of survival that relate to other disasters. Record that fact or story here.]

**CRITICAL THINKING**

# Self-Assessment

To get the most out of the *Above & Beyond* series, you need to take charge of your own progress in improving your reading comprehension and critical thinking skills. Here are some of the features that help you work on those essential skills.

**Reading Comprehension Exercises.** Complete these exercises immediately after reading the article. They help you recall what you have read, understand the stated and implied main ideas, and add words to your working vocabulary.

**Critical Thinking Skills Exercises.** These exercises help you focus on the author's approach and purpose, recognize and generate summaries and paraphrases, and identify relationships between ideas.

**Personal Response and Self-Assessment.** Questions in this category help you relate the articles to your personal experience and give you the opportunity to evaluate your understanding of the information in that lesson.

**Compare and Contrast Charts.** At the end of each unit you will complete a Compare and Contrast chart. The completed chart helps you see what the articles have in common and gives you an opportunity to explore your own ideas about the topics discussed in the articles.

**The Graphs.** The graphs and charts at the end of each unit enable you to keep track of your progress. Check your graphs regularly with your teacher. Decide whether your progress is satisfactory or whether you need additional work on some skills. What types of exercises are you having difficulty with? Talk with your teacher about ways to work on the skills in which you need the most practice.

# Unit One

# Lost on the Mountain

*A father and his son took the wrong trail at a ski resort in Turkey and discovered they were hopelessly lost.*

A cardinal rule of survival when you become lost is to stay right where you are. That makes it easier for a rescue party to find you. Air Force Lieutenant Colonel Mike Couillard knew the rule. He had attended a 17-day United States Air Force Survival Training Course. Yet on January 15, 1995, when Couillard and his 10-year-old son Matthew became lost while skiing in Turkey, he made the mistake of thinking he didn't need help. "I really thought we were going to find our way off the mountain," he said later. Instead, he kept on moving and ended up leading his son down the wrong side of the mountain. As a result of that crucial mistake, father and son spent the next nine and a half days battling to stay alive.

2    The Couillards became lost on what was supposed to be their last ski run of the day. It started snowing as they rode up the T-bar lift around 2:30 p.m. By the time they reached the 7,300-foot summit of Kartalkaya Mountain, the storm had turned into a raging blizzard. Visibility had dropped to almost nothing. Blinded by the snow, Couillard searched but couldn't find the ski trail. He decided they should just ski down the mountain and hope to find their way back to the ski lodge. Before long, he and Matthew were picking their way through dense stands of pine trees, turning left, then right, and then left again. By nightfall, they were exhausted and had found no trace of any trail, let alone the ski lodge. At that point, Couillard knew they would have to spend the night on the mountain. The two

of them began gathering tree branches to build a shelter from the wind and snow. As he later wrote in his book, *Miracle on the Mountain*, building the shelter was, in his mind, "the cutoff point that meant we were in a survival situation."

3    During that first night on the mountain, temperatures dropped below zero. The shelter helped, but it really provided only minimal protection. The next morning they got lucky: they found a small cave that was just large enough for the two of them. The cave protected them from the snow and the wind, but not the bitter cold. Matthew's toes were already turning white—a sure sign of frostbite. With weather conditions so bad, Couillard decided their best chance was to stay in the cave and wait for the skies to clear. But day after day passed, and the snow and wind continued.

4    Meanwhile, the Turkish and American authorities launched a massive search-and-rescue operation with 120 volunteers. The heavy snow hampered their efforts, though, and a dense fog made matters worse. More than four feet of snow fell during the first four days. Still, in moments when the storms did let up, helicopters made passes over the mountain. Unfortunately,

because Couillard and his son had skied down the wrong side of the mountain, they were outside of the search zone. The pilots never looked in the area of the cave. Three times, Couillard and Matthew saw the

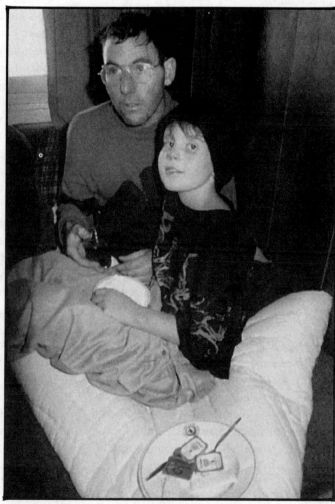

*Mike Couillard and his son huddled in a cave for days until they realized no one would come to find them.*

helicopters fly overhead, but despite their best efforts to call attention to themselves, the pilots never saw them. Matthew later said, each time a helicopter appeared and then disappeared, "you lose your hope all over again."

5   Back in Ankara, Turkey's capital city, Couillard's wife, Mary, and the couple's other two children waited anxiously for news. The lost father and son had attracted such widespread attention that all sorts of rumors began to sprout. One false claim came from a terrorist organization called "The Party of God." This group claimed it had kidnapped the two lost skiers and said it would kill them unless one of its jailed leaders was released from prison. The threat was plausible enough for *The New York Times* to run a story with the headline "2 Americans Reported Abducted in Turkey."

6   Back in their cave, Couillard and Matthew remained hostages to their environment. They had nothing to eat except for a handful of sweets and melted snow. After seven days, they were nearly starving to death. All hope of rescue was fading. Matthew suffered from such severe frostbite that he was unable to walk. Couillard began to feel reconciled to the notion that they would both soon be dead. Indeed, although neither of them was aware of it, the authorities had called off the entire rescue effort. By the seventh day of their

disappearance, all of the rescue teams assumed that the Couillards had not survived.

7   Huddled in the cave, his strength ebbing away, Mike Couillard faced a critical choice. He could either stay with Matthew and gradually freeze to death, or he could leave his son alone and ski down the mountain in one last effort to find help. "I hope I never face a decision that difficult again," said Couillard. He knew that rescue from search teams was extremely unlikely. Since Matthew could no longer walk or ski, the only real chance for them to get off the mountain alive was for Couillard to seek help alone. Thankful that the sky had cleared, Couillard said a heart-wrenching goodbye to his son and headed off. After a few hours, he came across some abandoned huts, but none of them were stored with food or tools. Too weak to go on, he spent a sleepless night in one of the huts, his mind filled with worried thoughts of Matthew.

8   The next day, Couillard did not have the energy to continue down the mountain or to return to his son, so he stayed in the hut. He then spent a second night in the hut. At last, on the third day there, Couillard heard the sound of an engine. Using his last bit of energy, he stumbled outside and shouted for help. The sound he heard had come from the engine of a truck that was carrying tree cutters. None of them

spoke any English, but Couillard spoke enough Turkish to guide them to the cave, and within an hour he was again holding Matthew—weak but alive—in his arms. The darkest, most stressful days of their lives were finally over.

9   Both father and son spent more than two months in the hospital recovering from their ordeal. Couillard needed a skin graft on his left foot. Matthew lost one toe and part of another from the frostbite on his right foot. "I feel like Lazarus in a lot of ways," said Mike Couillard, referencing a Biblical character that is brought back to life. "The world had basically given us up for dead. Now we are alive." ✳

*If you have been timed while reading this article, enter your reading time below. Then turn to the Words-per-Minute Table on page 55 and look up your reading speed (words per minute). Enter your reading speed on the graph on page 56.*

**Reading Time: Lesson 1**

_____ : _____
*Minutes*        *Seconds*

## A Finding the Main Idea

One statement below expresses the main idea of the article. One statement is too general, or too broad. The other statement explains only part of the article; it is too narrow. Label the statements using the following key:

**M—Main Idea**     **B—Too Broad**     **N—Too Narrow**

_____ 1. A father and his son became lost while skiing in a snowstorm.

_____ 2. Mike Couillard and his son Matthew were lost in a storm for almost 10 days while skiing in Turkey.

_____ 3. Mike Couillard and his son Matthew found a cave to protect them from the snow and the wind.

_____ Score 15 points for a correct M answer.

_____ Score 5 points for each correct B or N answer.

_____ **Total Score:** Finding the Main Idea

## B Recalling Facts

How well do you remember the facts in the article? Put an X in the box next to the answer that correctly completes each statement about the article.

1. During the first night on the mountain, Couillard and his son stayed in a
   ☐ a. shelter made of tree branches.
   ☐ b. cave.
   ☐ c. abandoned hut.

2. The rescue operation searched for the Couillards with
   ☐ a. dogs.
   ☐ b. helicopters.
   ☐ c. planes.

3. A terrorist organization claimed that it had
   ☐ a. found Couillard and his son in a cave.
   ☐ b. killed Couillard and his son.
   ☐ c. kidnapped Couillard and his son.

4. Mike Couillard was found by
   ☐ a. a helicopter rescue team.
   ☐ b. some tree-cutting workers.
   ☐ c. a band of Turkish skiers.

5. Mike Couillard spent two days and nights in the cabin because he
   ☐ a. expected to be rescued there.
   ☐ b. believed his son would come and join him.
   ☐ c. didn't have the energy to continue looking for help.

Score 5 points for each correct answer.

_____ **Total Score:** Recalling Facts

# C Making Inferences

When you combine your own experiences and information from a text to draw a conclusion that is not directly stated in that text, you are making an inference. Below are five statements that may or may not be inferences based on information in the article. Label the statements using the following key:

**C—Correct Inference**          **F—Faulty Inference**

_____ 1. Mike Couillard regretted his decision to try to find his way down the mountain rather than wait for a rescue party.

_____ 2. The side of the mountain the Couillards were skiing on was not part of the ski trail.

_____ 3. Couillard was sure the rescuers would find them alive eventually.

_____ 4. Couillard and his son would have found their way back to the ski lodge if they had been better skiers.

_____ 5. If Couillard had stayed in the cave with his son, there is a good chance he and his son would not have been rescued.

> Score 5 points for each correct answer.
>
> _____ **Total Score**: Making Inferences

# D Using Words Precisely

Each numbered sentence below contains an underlined word or phrase from the article. Following the sentence are three definitions. One definition is closest to the meaning of the underlined word. One definition is opposite or nearly opposite. Label those two definitions using the following key. Do not label the remaining definition.

**C—Closest**          **O—Opposite or Nearly Opposite**

1. A cardinal rule of survival when you become lost is to stay right where you are.

   _____ a. most important

   _____ b. natural

   _____ c. minor

2. As a result of that crucial mistake, father and son spent the next nine and a half days battling to stay alive.

   _____ a. unimportant, slight

   _____ b. critical, serious

   _____ c. unexpected

3. The heavy snow hampered the efforts of the search party.

   _____ a. assisted, helped

   _____ b. interfered with, got in the way of

   _____ c. forced

4. The terrorists' threat was plausible enough for *The New York Times* to run a story with the headline "2 Americans Reported Abducted in Turkey."

   _____ a. believable, possible

   _____ b. doubtful, unlikely

   _____ c. upsetting, disturbing

5. Couillard began to feel <u>reconciled to</u> the notion that they would both soon die.

_____ a. disagreeing with

_____ b. unaware of

_____ c. accepting of

_____ Score 3 points for each correct C answer.

_____ Score 2 points for each correct O answer.

_____ **Total Score**: Using Words Precisely

Enter the four total scores in the spaces below, and add them together to find your Reading Comprehension Score. Then record your score on the graph on page 57.

| Score | Question Type | Lesson 1 |
|---|---|---|
| _____ | Finding the Main Idea | |
| _____ | Recalling Facts | |
| _____ | Making Inferences | |
| _____ | Using Words Precisely | |
| _____ | **Reading Comprehension Score** | |

## Author's Approach

Put an X in the box next to the correct answer.

1. The main purpose of the first paragraph is to

☐ a. summarize the experience of Mike Couillard and his son.

☐ b. describe Couillard's survival training course.

☐ c. relate the rules of survival.

2. From the statements below, choose the one that you believe the author would agree with.

☐ a. Skiing in Turkey is very dangerous.

☐ b. Mike Couillard was partly to blame for becoming lost.

☐ c. Helicopters are not very useful in search operations.

3. What does the author mean by the statement "Couillard and Matthew remained hostages to their environment"?

☐ a. The weather conditions forced them to stay in the cave.

☐ b. Someone held the father and son captive in the cave.

☐ c. Couillard and his son were being held for ransom.

4. Considering the statement from the article "As a result of that crucial mistake, father and son spent the next nine and a half days battling to stay alive," you can conclude that the author wants the reader to think that

☐ a. Couillard and his son were very unlucky.

☐ b. Couillard made a bad mistake, but everyone makes mistakes.

☐ c. Couillard's mistake might have been the last one he ever made.

_____ Number of correct answers

Record your personal assessment of your work on the Critical Thinking Chart on page 58.

CRITICAL THINKING

# Summarizing and Paraphrasing

Put an X in the box next to the correct answer for questions 1 and 2. Follow the directions provided for question 3.

1. Read the statement from the article below. Then read the paraphrase of that statement. Choose the reason that best tells why the paraphrase does not say the same thing as the statement.

    Statement:  By nightfall, they were exhausted and had found no trace of any trail, let alone the ski lodge.

    Paraphrase:  By sunset, they were tired from following the trail, but they had not found the ski lodge.

    ☐  a.  Paraphrase says too much.

    ☐  b.  Paraphrase doesn't say enough.

    ☐  c.  Paraphrase doesn't agree with the statement.

2. Below are summaries of the article. Choose the summary that says all the most important things about the article but in the fewest words.

    ☐  a.  Couillard and his son became lost, but they were rescued.

    ☐  b.  Couillard and his son became lost for 10 days while skiing in Turkey. They took shelter in a cave. Couillard left to look for help, and the two were saved.

    ☐  c.  Couillard and his son became lost because Couillard tried to ski down a mountain in a blizzard. They were eventually saved by Turkish tree cutters.

3. Reread paragraph 3 in the article. Below, write a summary of the paragraph in no more than 25 words.

    _____

    _____

    _____

    _____

    _____

Reread your summary and decide whether it covers the important ideas in the paragraph. Next, decide how to shorten the summary to 15 words or less without leaving out any essential information. Write this summary below.

_____

_____

_____

_____

_____ Number of correct answers

Record your personal assessment of your work on the Critical Thinking Chart on page 58.

# Critical Thinking

Put an X in the box next to the correct answer for questions 1, 3, and 4. Follow the directions provided for the other questions.

1. From what the article told about Mike Couillard and his son, you can predict that on their next ski trip they will

    ☐  a.  ski only on mountains in the United States.

    ☐  b.  make sure they know exactly where the trail and ski lodge are.

    ☐  c.  bring food, blankets, and sleeping bags with them.

2. Choose from the letters below to correctly complete the following statement. Write the letters on the lines.

    According to the article, _____ caused Couillard to _____, and the effect was _____.

    a.  hearing the sound of an engine

    b.  he was found by some tree cutters

    c.  call for help

3. Into which of the following categories would this article best fit?

☐ a. profiles of sports heroes

☐ b. reports of amazing but true stories

☐ c. articles about winter games

4. If you were a member of a rescue party, how could you use the information in the article to find someone who was lost?

☐ a. Expand the search area, realizing that people tend to wander from their original area.

☐ b. Use more helicopters.

☐ c. Delay the start of the search and give the lost person more time to find a way out.

5. In which paragraph did you find your information or details to answer question 2?

_____

_____ Number of correct answers

Record your personal assessment of your work on the Critical Thinking Chart on page 58.

## Personal Response

What was most surprising or interesting to you about this article?

_____

_____

_____

_____

## Self-Assessment

One good question about this article that was not asked would be

_____

_____

_____

_____

and the answer is

_____

_____

_____

_____

_____

CRITICAL THINKING

# Adrift at Sea

*Mexican fishermen Salvador Ordóñez, Lucio Rendón, and Jesús Vidaña survived nine months lost at sea.*

When the group of Taiwanese fishermen navigated their boat through the waters near the Marshall Islands on August 9, 2006, they weren't expecting to meet anyone. After all, they were in the middle of the Pacific Ocean, about halfway between Hawaii and Australia. Out there, the only thing anyone might have expected to see was a whale or some other sea mammal momentarily coming to the surface for air. To the fishermen's surprise, what they saw was not a whale but rather a 25-foot boat, drifting silently. On board were three exhausted men—Jesús Vidaña, Lucio Rendón, and Salvador Ordóñez—who had been missing and presumed dead. In fact, the last time anyone had seen them was nine months ago and 5,000 miles away, off the western coast of Mexico!

2 When Vidaña, Rendón, and Ordóñez were brought ashore, they were inundated with questions. Some people thought it was impossible for their boat to have drifted that far. Others wondered why the men were in such good physical condition and showed few signs of illness from lack of food and water. Not only that, there had originally been five people on the boat, but now there were only three. What had happened to the other two? Had the three killed their missing companions and eaten the bodies to stay alive? Or was the whole event a hoax to attract attention? It took weeks for the story to untangle, and although media theories ran wild for a while, the truth turned out to be pretty wild all by itself.

3 The saga began when two wealthy Mexicans, known as Señor Juan and El Farsero, approached Vidaña, Rendón, and Ordóñez in the town of San Blas, Mexico. Señor Juan owned a boat; he and El Farsero hired the three men to take them shark fishing in the Pacific Ocean. "The three of us, we are real fishermen," said Vidaña of himself, Rendón, and Ordóñez. "We were born fishermen. We are used to bad weather, the sun, and working hard." Ordóñez had a few misgivings about the trip, mostly because he didn't think Señor Juan had brought enough supplies for the boat. "I was worried, and told him it was too little food, too little water, too little petrol," Ordóñez recalls. "I thought about not going, but my need was great. I needed a few extra dollars."

4 Early in the morning of October 28, 2005, the five men set out, and by afternoon they were 60 miles offshore. After throwing out their long line to catch bait for sharks, the men settled in to rest, expecting to pull the line in later that day. As they dozed, however, the sea turned rough. The line and its buoys—worth about $1,000—broke. When the men awoke and realized what had happened, Señor Juan insisted that they search for the line. He kept them searching long into the night until eventually the boat ran out of gas. Like many fishermen in that region, Vidaña, Rendón and Ordóñez carried only the necessary fishing equipment. They had no cell phones, radio, or GPS unit. Still, they could see lights from other boats, and they fully expected one of them would come close enough so they could call out to

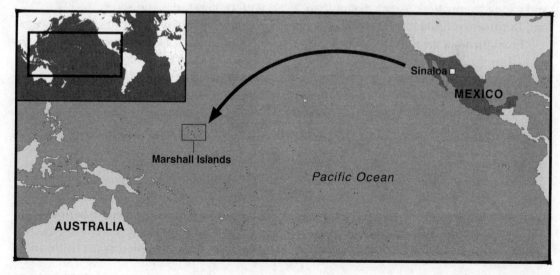

The fishing boat was carried by winds and currents more than 5,500 miles across nearly the entire Pacific Ocean.

the crew. Unfortunately, they never got the chance. Instead, a strong wind picked up, which lasted several days, and it carried the five men farther and farther out into the Pacific Ocean.

5    After two weeks of drifting, the five men had run out of food and water and were growing progressively weaker. Ordóñez remembers thinking, "I am going to die unless I do something." He was so desperately thirsty, he began drinking his own urine. His friends Rendón and Vidaña did the same. Señor Juan and El Farsero, however, refused to follow their example, preferring instead to suffer thirst. A couple of days later, when a large sea turtle swam past their boat, Ordóñez jumped into the water, grabbed hold of it, and hoisted it into the boat. He and Rendón killed it, then they and Vidaña consumed it, drinking its blood and eating its raw flesh. Again, Señor Juan and El Farsero refused to join them.

6    From then on, the three fishermen gained strength, while Señor Juan and El Farsero became weaker. The five men shared the rainwater they collected during storms, but except for that, Señor Juan and El Farsero declined to take any nourishment. Vidaña, Rendón, and Ordóñez crafted hooks out of springs from the boat's motors and used them to catch fish. From time to time they were also able to grab birds that landed on their boat. They didn't always have food. There was one 13-day period when all they caught was one seabird. Mostly, however,

they were able to keep hunger away. Whenever they did catch something, they ate it raw—and they ate every bit of it. "We would eat everything of the birds we caught, even the bones," Vidaña said. They always offered portions to Señor Juan and El Farsero, but neither one ever accepted.

7    Over the next two months, the boat was rocked by storms so fierce the men thought it would sink. "We really thought we were going to die," recalls Rendón of one extremely bad storm. To stabilize the rocking vessel and keep it afloat, Ordóñez tied hollow containers to the sides. He also strung rope through a large cloth to make a rudimentary sail to help them steer. During the storms and also during the endless hours in between, he kept the others calm by reading aloud from his Bible. At other times, they entertained each other performing stories and songs.

8    In late January, Señor Juan began vomiting blood. By this time, he and El Farsero were barely conscious and lay curled up in the corners of the boat. Eight days later, Señor Juan died. El Farsero held on for three more weeks. In both cases, Vidaña, Rendón, and Ordóñez waited a respectful three days and then dumped their bodies into the ocean.

9    By August 2006, the boat had drifted to within 200 miles of the Marshall Islands. That is where the Taiwanese fishermen found them. After many interviews, the men's story was accepted as the truth, and

Vidaña, Rendón, and Ordóñez were allowed to go home.

10    When they returned, the men were hounded by movie producers and media agents looking for them to sell their story. Their families, who had given them up for dead, struggled with the unwanted outside attention. The local people were divided over suspicion that they had made up their story, and some were jealous of their fame. In addition, there were rumors they might be offered large sums of money for their story. The men worried that kidnappers would target them to collect big ransoms. Vidaña, Rendón, and Ordóñez found that their lives had changed. It seemed that coming home was in some ways almost as challenging as being adrift at sea. ✳

*If you have been timed while reading this article, enter your reading time below. Then turn to the Words-per-Minute Table on page 55 and look up your reading speed (words per minute). Enter your reading speed on the graph on page 56.*

**Reading Time: Lesson 2**

_____ : _____
*Minutes         Seconds*

## A Finding the Main Idea

One statement below expresses the main idea of the article. One statement is too general, or too broad. The other statement explains only part of the article; it is too narrow. Label the statements using the following key:

**M—Main Idea**     **B—Too Broad**     **N—Too Narrow**

_____ 1. A boat with three Mexican fishermen was found by a group of fishermen.

_____ 2. Three Mexican fishermen survived after being lost at sea for more than nine months.

_____ 3. Three Mexican fishermen adrift on the ocean survived by eating what they could catch.

_____ Score 15 points for a correct M answer.

_____ Score 5 points for each correct B or N answer.

_____ **Total Score**: Finding the Main Idea

## B Recalling Facts

How well do you remember the facts in the article? Put an X in the box next to the answer that correctly completes each statement about the article.

1. The five men set off on their fishing trip in
   ☐ a. October 2005.
   ☐ b. January 2006.
   ☐ c. August 2006.

2. The boat ran out of gas because the men
   ☐ a. searched all night for their fishing line.
   ☐ b. went out too far.
   ☐ c. forgot to fill the tank before they left.

3. Two of the men died because
   ☐ a. the fishermen refused to share their food.
   ☐ b. they were injured during one of the storms.
   ☐ c. they refused to eat the raw meat.

4. The first man to die was
   ☐ a. Lucio Rendón.
   ☐ b. Señor Juan
   ☐ c. El Farsero.

5. The boat was found when it had drifted to within 200 miles of
   ☐ a. Hawaii.
   ☐ b. Mexico.
   ☐ c. the Marshall Islands.

Score 5 points for each correct answer.

_____ **Total Score**: Recalling Facts

## C | Making Inferences

When you combine your own experiences and information from a text to draw a conclusion that is not directly stated in that text, you are making an inference. Below are five statements that may or may not be inferences based on information in the article. Label the statements using the following key:

**C—Correct Inference**          **F—Faulty Inference**

_____  1.  Many other Mexican fishermen have been swept far off course by storms and never made it back home.

_____  2.  Señor Juan and El Farsero kept looking for the fishing line because it was so expensive.

_____  3.  Vidaña, Rendón, and Ordóñez always chose not to carry cell phones, a radio, or GPS units when they went fishing.

_____  4.  The three survivors believed they would eventually find land or another boat.

_____  5.  Vidaña, Rendón, and Ordóñez enjoyed all the attention they received when they returned home to Mexico.

---

Score 5 points for each correct answer.

_____ **Total Score**: Making Inferences

---

## D | Using Words Precisely

Each numbered sentence below contains an underlined word or phrase from the article. Following the sentence are three definitions. One definition is closest to the meaning of the underlined word. One definition is opposite or nearly opposite. Label those two definitions using the following key. Do not label the remaining definition.

**C—Closest**          **O—Opposite or Nearly Opposite**

1.  Whales momentarily come to the surface of the water for air.

    _____  a.  noisily

    _____  b.  permanently

    _____  c.  for a short time

2.  When Vidaña, Rendón, and Ordóñez were brought ashore, they were inundated with questions.

    _____  a.  left alone

    _____  b.  overwhelmed, taken over

    _____  c.  criticized

3.  Ordóñez had a few misgivings about the trip, mostly because he didn't think the boat had enough supplies.

    _____  a.  doubts, concerns

    _____  b.  positive feelings

    _____  c.  complaints

4.  To stabilize the vessel and keep it afloat, Ordóñez tied hollow containers to the sides.

    _____  a.  watch over

    _____  b.  balance, make level

    _____  c.  tilt, wobble

5. He strung rope through a large cloth to make a <u>rudimentary</u> sail to help them steer.

_____ a. complicated

_____ b. strong

_____ c. basic, simple

---

_____ Score 3 points for each correct C answer.

_____ Score 2 points for each correct O answer.

_____ **Total Score**: Using Words Precisely

---

Enter the four total scores in the spaces below, and add them together to find your Reading Comprehension Score. Then record your score on the graph on page 57.

| Score | Question Type | Lesson 2 |
|---|---|---|
| _____ | Finding the Main Idea | |
| _____ | Recalling Facts | |
| _____ | Making Inferences | |
| _____ | Using Words Precisely | |
| _____ | **Reading Comprehension Score** | |

## Author's Approach

Put an X in the box next to the correct answer.

1. The author probably wrote this article in order to
   - ☐ a. shock readers by telling what men will do to survive.
   - ☐ b. scare readers from ever going on a fishing trip.
   - ☐ c. inform readers about an incredible tale of survival.

2. The author tells this story mainly by
   - ☐ a. providing a diary-like coverage of their nine-month ordeal.
   - ☐ b. questioning whether the three men were truthful or not.
   - ☐ c. describing the events of the experience in sequence.

3. What does the author imply by saying "Others wondered why the men were in such good physical condition and showed few signs of illness from lack of food and water"?
   - ☐ a. Because the men were in such good shape, people assumed they were lying about their experience.
   - ☐ b. The people thought the fishermen looked better when they came back than when they left.
   - ☐ c. The people admired how physically fit the fishermen were.

4. Considering the statement from the article "Their families struggled with the attention," you can conclude that the author wants the reader to think that the families
   - ☐ a. fought with each other for attention.
   - ☐ b. were not used to attention and had a hard time with it.
   - ☐ c. wanted the attention of the movie producers and reporters.

---

_____ Number of correct answers

Record your personal assessment of your work on the Critical Thinking Chart on page 58.

**CRITICAL THINKING**

# Summarizing and Paraphrasing

Follow the directions provided for questions 1 and 3. Put an X in the box next to the correct answer for question 2.

1. Complete the following one-sentence summary of the article using the lettered phrases from the phrase bank below. Write the letters on the lines.

**Phrase Bank:**

a. the men's survival at sea

b. the finding of the boat

c. the men returning to Mexico

The article, "Adrift at Sea" begins with _____, goes on to describe _____, and ends with _____.

2. Choose the sentence that correctly restates the following sentence from the article: "As they dozed, however, the sea turned rough."

☐ a.   While the men slept, the ocean became choppy.

☐ b.   The waves grew higher, but the men still did not wake up.

☐ c.   The longer they rested, the rougher the sea became.

3. Reread the first paragraph of the article. Below, write a summary of the paragraph in no more than 25 words.

_____

_____

_____

_____

_____

_____

Reread your summary and decide whether it covers the important ideas in the paragraph. Next, decide how to shorten the summary to 15 words or less without leaving out any essential information. Write this summary below.

_____

_____

_____

_____

_____ Number of correct answers

Record your personal assessment of your work on the Critical Thinking Chart on page 58.

# Critical Thinking

Follow the directions provided for questions 1, 2, and 5. Put an X in the box next to the correct answer for the other questions.

1. Choose from the letters below to correctly complete the following statement. Write the letters on the lines.

On the positive side, _____, but on the negative side, _____.

a.   the men carried only the necessary fishing equipment

b.   the men's lives became more complicated

c.   the three fishermen survived and were rescued

2. Choose from the letters below to correctly complete the following statement. Write the letters on the lines.

According to the article, _____ caused Señor Juan and El Farsero to _____, and the effect was _____.

a.   grow weaker

b.   refusing to eat raw meat

c.   they died

3. How is "Adrift at Sea" an example of the theme of *Survivors*?

☐ a. The media people thought the story of the fishermen's survival would make good entertainment.

☐ b. The three men were lucky to survive on the boat for nine months.

☐ c. Despite being lost at sea, these three men kept trying and found creative ways to survive.

4. From the information in paragraph 6, you can conclude that the fishermen were

☐ a. used to eating raw meat.

☐ b. very glad to eat the raw meat.

☐ c. disgusted that they had to eat raw meat.

5. Which paragraphs provide evidence that supports your answer to question 2?

_____

_____ Number of correct answers

Record your personal assessment of your work on the Critical Thinking Chart on page 58.

## Personal Response

I can't believe

_____

_____

_____

_____

## Self-Assessment

I was confused about question _____ in _____ section because

_____

_____

_____

_____

_____

_____

_____

_____

**CRITICAL THINKING**

# Life Rolls On

*Jesse Billauer sustained a spinal cord injury while surfing, so now he rides a specially designed surfboard.*

What would you do if all your dreams for the future were suddenly snatched away from you? How would you react if one minute you were on top of the world, looking forward to a life of doing what you loved . . . but the next minute you found yourself lying flat on your back, permanently unable to move? Most of us will never have to really answer these questions. For Jesse Billauer, however, these questions became the central focus of his life when, at the age of 17, he suffered an accident that left him paralyzed from the chest down.

2  Billauer grew up in the beach town of Pacific Palisades, California, where he excelled in baseball, soccer, and floor hockey. At the age of nine, he tried surfing for the first time and quickly fell in love with the sport. His desire to surf was so strong that he lost the urge to play any other sports. By the time he was 11, Billauer was surfing for prizes. He had a natural talent, and as he got better, he gained people's attention. His image began appearing in a variety of surfing magazines too. Soon, major manufacturers started calling him to sponsor his surfing competitions. He surfed in competitions in Indonesia, Tahiti, and Hawaii. It seemed he was being carried on a never-ending wave to stardom. By early 1996, Billauer was named as one of the world's top 100 up-and-coming surfers. He was on the verge of joining the professional tour when his dream of stardom suddenly was wiped out.

3  On March 25, 1996, Billauer and two friends waded out into the ocean with their surfboards. They planned to catch a few waves before school. "It was a 6-to-8-foot day," Billauer remembered. He caught a wave and confidently tucked himself inside "the tube" as the lip of the wave crested over his head. Usually a wave collapses behind a surfer, but this wave unpredictably crashed directly onto Billauer's back. It pushed him down—straight through the shallow water and into a sandbar. Immediately, his body went limp. Billauer found himself helplessly floating face down in the water and unable to turn over. He might easily have drowned if he had panicked. But Billauer held his breath and waited to be rescued by one of his friends or by another wave. Luckily, a few moments later, a new wave flipped him over on his back. This allowed him to catch his breath again and then yell for help. At first his friends thought Billauer was fooling around. When they realized he wasn't, they pulled him out of the water and onto the beach.

4  Billauer was transported by helicopter to the UCLA Medical Center. The doctors there determined that his spinal cord had been injured at the C-6 level, meaning the sixth vertebra of the neck. Billauer was paralyzed from the middle of his chest down. He had no sensation or movement below mid-chest and only limited use of his arms and hands. The life that Jesse Billauer had always known was over, and a new life was about to begin.

*Professional surfer Sunny Garcia helps Jesse Billauer after competing in the "They Will Surf Again" Expression Session Men's Finals.*

5 Finding a way to survive such an extreme change in lifestyle was enormously difficult at first. Jesse Billauer, however, is a unique individual. He certainly had his bleak moments, but visiting with friends and sharing fond memories of riding the waves always cheered him up. Surfing had brought Billauer extreme joy, and he very much wanted to experience that joy again.

6 "Jesse's desire to surf again was a burning desire," one friend later said. "He would surf again at any cost." Billauer received encouragement from many of his friends, most notably from surfing stars Kelly Slater and Rob Machado. They agreed to help him realize his new dream. First, Billauer arranged for a surfboard maker to build him a custom surfboard. The special board was thicker and wider than an average surfboard. It also had special straps and an extra rocker, or curve, in the front to keep the board's nose out of the water. The idea was that Billauer would lie on the board on his stomach and prop himself up on his elbows. He would control the board's direction by shifting his weight from one side to the other. While the board was being made, Billauer built up his strength and gained as much mobility as he could through physical therapy.

7 Finally, after three years, the day arrived when Billauer would return to the ocean. His friends strapped him onto his custom-built surfboard, and Machado towed Billauer out into the surf and guided him into a small wave. It was a great victory for Billauer for two reasons: Not only could he control the board by himself but he also achieved a high personal goal. During the next three hours, as the group of friends happily rode the waves, Billauer imagined how surfing could always be an important part of his life.

8 Billauer knew he could always rely on his friends to help him surf, but he wanted more than that. He wanted to share his victory with other spinal cord victims. He wanted to help them experience the freedom and joy of surfing—or whatever sport they loved. To achieve that goal, he founded a non-profit organization called Life Rolls On. Its mission is to promote adaptive sports for young people with spinal cord injuries. Billauer hoped his organization could pave the way for others to set goals and attain them in the same way he had.

9 As part of Life Rolls On, Billauer set up a special program called They Will Surf Again. The program organizes events in which volunteers help persons with spinal cord injuries get back into the water and surf. Every year, They Will Surf Again holds surfing events at various places around the country. In 2009, for example, the location was La Jolla, California. More than 150 volunteers gathered at a beach to assist about four dozen paralyzed surfers. One of these was six-year-old Ian McFarland.

His spinal cord had been injured in a car accident that killed both of his parents. His father had taught him to surf, and thanks to Billauer's program, he believed he could do it again. Supporters cheered when McFarland was taken into the water on his surfboard and he rolled over the waves for the first time since he lost the use of his legs.

10 In late 2009 Life Rolls On joined with the Christopher and Dana Reeve Foundation. With this deal came more financial and marketing clout for Billauer's projects, and his organization expanded to include They Will Ski Again and They Will Skate Again events. As Billauer said of the partnership, "We can inspire even more people with the message that life after spinal cord injury truly 'rolls on.'" ✷

*If you have been timed while reading this article, enter your reading time below. Then turn to the Words-per-Minute Table on page 55 and look up your reading speed (words per minute). Enter your reading speed on the graph on page 56.*

**Reading Time: Lesson 3**

_____ : _____
*Minutes*      *Seconds*

# A Finding the Main Idea

One statement below expresses the main idea of the article. One statement is too general, or too broad. The other statement explains only part of the article; it is too narrow. Label the statements using the following key:

**M—Main Idea**     **B—Too Broad**     **N—Too Narrow**

_____  1. After he was paralyzed, surfer Jesse Billauer founded Life Rolls On, an organization that promotes sports for young people with spinal cord injuries.

_____  2. Jesse Billauer competed in surfing competitions before he became paralyzed in an accident.

_____  3. Most people with spinal cord injuries are not able to participate in the sports they used to enjoy.

_____ Score 15 points for a correct M answer.

_____ Score 5 points for each correct B or N answer.

_____ **Total Score**: Finding the Main Idea

# B Recalling Facts

How well do you remember the facts in the article? Put an X in the box next to the answer that correctly completes each statement about the article.

1. Billauer started surfing when he was
   - ☐ a.  9 years old.
   - ☐ b.  11 years old.
   - ☐ c.  17 years old.

2. Billauer's surfing competitions took him to Indonesia, Tahiti, and
   - ☐ a.  Mexico.
   - ☐ b.  Australia.
   - ☐ c.  Hawaii.

3. Billauer became paralyzed in a
   - ☐ a.  surfing accident.
   - ☐ b.  skating accident.
   - ☐ c.  car accident.

4. Rob Machado
   - ☐ a.  provided the idea for Life Rolls On.
   - ☐ b.  built Billauer's custom surfboard.
   - ☐ c.  helped Billauer to surf for the first time since the accident.

5. In September 2009, They Will Surf Again held an event in
   - ☐ a.  Pacific Palisades, California.
   - ☐ b.  La Jolla, California.
   - ☐ c.  Los Angeles, California.

Score 5 points for each correct answer.

_____ **Total Score**: Recalling Facts

## C Making Inferences

When you combine your own experiences and information from a text to draw a conclusion that is not directly stated in that text, you are making an inference. Below are five statements that may or may not be inferences based on information in the article. Label the statements using the following key:

**C—Correct Inference**          **F—Faulty Inference**

_____  1.  Very few people with spinal cord injuries want to participate in sports.

_____  2.  If Billauer had been taken to a hospital more quickly for treatment, his paralysis would have been much less serious.

_____  3.  Many people with spinal cord injuries have been inspired by Jesse Billauer's life.

_____  4.  Billauer's accident was caused by his carelessness.

_____  5.  Surfing can be a dangerous sport.

---

Score 5 points for each correct answer.

_____ **Total Score**: Making Inferences

---

## D Using Words Precisely

Each numbered sentence below contains an underlined word or phrase from the article. Following the sentence are three definitions. One definition is closest to the meaning of the underlined word. One definition is opposite or nearly opposite. Label those two definitions using the following key. Do not label the remaining definition.

**C—Closest**          **O—Opposite or Nearly Opposite**

1.  He caught a wave and confidently tucked himself inside "the tube," as the lip of the wave <u>crested</u> over his head.

_____  a.  smashed

_____  b.  hit bottom

_____  c.  reached its highest point

2.  He certainly had his <u>bleak</u> moments, but visiting with friends and sharing fond memories of riding the waves always cheered him up.

_____  a.  cheerful, pleasant

_____  b.  depressing, dismal

_____  c.  special, memorable

3.  First, Billauer arranged for a surfboard maker to build him a <u>custom</u> surfboard.

_____  a.  any size or shape

_____  b.  colorful

_____  c.  made according to specific details

4.  While the board was being made, Billauer built up his strength and gained as much <u>mobility</u> as he could through physical therapy.

_____  a.  confidence, assurance

_____  b.  flexibility, ability to move

_____  c.  rigidity, stiffness

5. With this deal came more financial and marketing <u>clout</u> for Billauer's projects.

_____ a. weakness

_____ b. influence, authority

_____ c. competition

_____ Score 3 points for each correct C answer.

_____ Score 2 points for each correct O answer.

_____ **Total Score**: Using Words Precisely

Enter the four total scores in the spaces below, and add them together to find your Reading Comprehension Score. Then record your score on the graph on page 57.

| Score | Question Type | Lesson 3 |
|-------|---------------|----------|
| _____ | Finding the Main Idea | |
| _____ | Recalling Facts | |
| _____ | Making Inferences | |
| _____ | Using Words Precisely | |
| _____ | **Reading Comprehension Score** | |

## Author's Approach

Put an X in the box next to the correct answer.

1. The main purpose of the first paragraph is to

☐ a. make the reader think about the questions that Billauer faced when he became paralyzed.

☐ b. describe how Billauer became paralyzed.

☐ c. inform the reader about Billauer's early life.

2. What is the author's purpose in writing this article?

☐ a. to persuade the reader to take up surfing

☐ b. to encourage the reader to learn more about spinal cord injuries

☐ c. to inform the reader about the inspiring life of Jesse Billauer

3. Judging by statements from the article "Life Rolls On," you can conclude that the author wants the reader to think that

☐ a. Billauer feels sorry for himself.

☐ b. Billauer's goal of helping young people with spinal cord injuries is not realistic.

☐ c. Billauer is a very generous man.

4. In this article, "Jesse's desire to surf again was a burning desire," means

☐ a. His desire to surf again was always present and taking his attention.

☐ b. He wanted to surf again, but felt deep pain knowing he would never be able to surf the way he used to.

☐ c. He wanted to surf again like he used to do.

_____ Number of correct answers

Record your personal assessment of your work on the Critical Thinking Chart on page 58.

**CRITICAL THINKING**

# Summarizing and Paraphrasing

Follow the directions provided for questions 1 and 3. Put an X in the box next to the correct answer for question 2.

1.  Look for the important ideas and events in paragraphs 3 and 4. Summarize those paragraphs in one or two sentences.

    _____

    _____

    _____

    _____

2.  Choose the sentence that correctly restates the following sentence from the article: "His desire to surf was so strong that he lost the urge to play any other sports."

    ☐ a.   He spent so much time surfing, he didn't have time to play any other sports.

    ☐ b.   He wanted to surf more than he wanted to play any other sport.

    ☐ c.   The only sport he liked any more was surfing.

3.  Reread paragraph 8 in the article. Below, write a summary of the paragraph in no more than 25 words.

    _____

    _____

    _____

    _____

    _____

    _____

    _____

    _____

Reread your summary and decide whether it covers the important ideas in the paragraph. Next, decide how to shorten the summary to 15 words or less without leaving out any essential information. Write this summary below.

_____

_____

_____

_____

_____ Number of correct answers

Record your personal assessment of your work on the Critical Thinking Chart on page 58.

# Critical Thinking

Put an X in the box next to the correct answer for questions 1, 2, 4, and 5. Follow the directions provided for question 3.

1.  Which of the following statements from the article is an opinion rather than a fact?

    ☐ a.   "Billauer was paralyzed from the middle of his chest down."

    ☐ b.   "Billauer was transported by helicopter to the UCLA Medical Center."

    ☐ c.   "Jesse Billauer, however, is a unique individual."

2.  Using the information in paragraphs 7 and 8, how would you define *adaptive sports*?

    ☐ a.   "sports that have loose rules and no competition."

    ☐ b.   "sports that are changed to meet the needs of persons with disabilities."

    ☐ c.   "sports that were created by Jesse Billauer."

**CRITICAL THINKING**

3. Reread paragraph 4. Then choose from the letters below to correctly complete the following statement. Write the letters on the lines.

According to paragraph 4, _____ because _____.

a. Billauer's spinal cord had been injured

b. the C-6 level of the spinal cord is in the neck

c. Billauer was paralyzed

4. From what the article told about Jesse Billauer, you can conclude that he

☐ a. wishes he had never begun surfing

☐ b. would like to do more to help people with spinal cord injuries.

☐ c. expects to get rich from his Life Rolls On foundation.

5. What did you have to do to answer question 3?

☐ a. find a cause (why something happened) and an effect (something that happened)

☐ b. find an opinion (what someone thinks about something)

☐ c. draw a conclusion (a sensible statement based on the text and your experience)

_____ Number of correct answers

Record your personal assessment of your work on the Critical Thinking Chart on page 58.

## Personal Response

How do you think Jesse Billauer felt the first time he went surfing after his accident?

_____

_____

_____

_____

## Self-Assessment

The part I found most difficult about the article was

_____

_____

_____

_____

I found this difficult because

_____

_____

_____

_____

CRITICAL THINKING

# Stranded!

*When the stranded divers reached a deserted island they met up with a Komodo dragon.*

The first two days of her three-day scuba diving adventure left Charlotte Allin awestruck. The 24-year-old British woman was dazzled by the astonishing beauty of Indonesia's coral reefs. She had a great time exploring this underwater paradise, which is home to a quarter of the world's known marine species. But it was the third day of the adventure—June 5, 2008—that Allin will remember for the rest of her life.

2    At about 3:00 in the afternoon, she and her friend James Manning were joined by Kathleen Mitchinson, who ran a local diving center and was the organizer of the trip. A French diver named Laurent Pinel and a Swedish diver named Helena Neradairen also joined them. All five were experienced scuba divers. They had to be because these waters, located between the Pacific and Indian oceans, are well-known for their strong and unpredictable "washing machine" currents.

3    At 4:10 P.M., the five divers returned to the surface as scheduled. They were only about 100 feet away from the dive boat, but for some reason, the boat was turned around, and the crew was facing the other way. The crew didn't see the divers. As the powerful current pushed them farther and farther away, the stunned divers shouted and blew whistles to attract the crew's attention. Soon, however, the five were left alone—stranded in shark-infested waters.

4    The companions could see nearby tiny islands, and they tried desperately to swim to them. Each time, just as they got close to land, the powerful current pushed them away, so that all they could do was swim in circles around it. They also spied a few fishing boats in the distance, but their shouts and whistles caused no reaction. By 6 P.M., and with darkness settling in, Allin said "we knew that we were in trouble." Rough waves crashed over them. They were physically exhausted from swimming and fighting the current, and they were getting cold also.

5    Then, around 7:30 P.M., they saw something in the water near them. "I actually thought it was the fin of a shark or a dolphin or something," recalls Allin. In fact, it was a six-foot log, and it was thick enough to support the five companions. The divers swam hard for the log and held on tight. As the water grew colder, the five huddled together for warmth and prepared to wait out the night. They threw off the heaviest pieces of their diving equipment and kept each other awake by talking and telling stories. Neradairen was extremely seasick, and they were all suffering from leg cramps.

6    At about 10:45 P.M., the wind dropped, and the sea finally calmed down. Around midnight, Manning and Mitchinson spotted the outline of another nearby island in the moonlight and decided to try and swim to it. As the two drew near, they were almost slammed against the rocks by the pounding surf. Mitchinson gave up and swam back to the log, but Manning kept going and finally made it through the rocky island barrier. Manning then swam back to the others and led them through the safe route to the island. After nine hours in the water, the five shivering divers crawled onto the beach, collapsed on the sand, and slept.

7    At sunrise the next morning, they awoke freezing cold. None of them knew where they had landed, but they hoped they were on Pandaua Island, which sometimes had fishing boats moored offshore. Actually, they were sitting on parched and deserted Rinca Island. Manning, a former commando who had served in Iraq and Afghanistan,

*The five divers were taken to safety after being stranded in the ocean.*

shed his wetsuit and set out to explore the island. He hoped to find people or perhaps some source of food. As far as they knew, they might be stranded for weeks. Manning's scouting mission might give them a chance for survival. Clad only in his wetsuit vest, shorts, and thin rubber diving boots, Manning climbed over the steep cliffs that bordered the coastline. At one point near the top of a cliff, a snake suddenly slithered in front of him, causing him to jump back and almost fall. Then he pushed back a branch and came close to disturbing a huge bee colony. "If the branch had hit them they would have gone berserk. It terrified me much more than the snake," said Manning.

8    Back at the beach, the others were suffering from the lack of food and water. By midday, Allin later recalled, their thirst was "terrible." Her lips were "swollen and white." The tropical sun was beating down on their island, which had some trees but very little shade. For food and some much-needed protein, they ate mussels that they scraped off the rocks. They tried to start a fire using a magnifying glass that Mitchinson had in her diving gear, but all they could produce was smoke. Some of them rolled large white rocks to form the letters "SOS" on a hillside in hopes of attracting a passing boat.

9    In the late afternoon, a huge Komodo dragon sauntered onto the beach. The Komodo dragon is the world's largest lizard, and can grow up to 10 feet long. With its razor-sharp teeth and claws and poisonous saliva, the Komodo dragon easily can kill whatever it can catch, and it will devour anything from a monkey to a water buffalo, including a human. When they saw the dragon, it had Manning's abandoned wetsuit in its mouth. The companions threw rocks, sticks, and even a heavy diving belt at the dragon to drive it away, but the muscular Komodo didn't give up very quickly. At one point, the creature almost bit Neradairen in the head when it snatched at her wetsuit hood lying in the sand next to her.

10    Meanwhile, Manning was struggling to get back to the beach. He went around the island, mostly by clambering over rocks, but when the rocks became too steep or dangerous to climb he swam. The water route generally was more perilous than climbing the cliffs, though, because at any moment, a wave might have bowled him into the jagged rocks. His energy spent, Manning knew he wouldn't make it back to the others before sunset, so he stretched out on a flat rock and closed his eyes for the night. The four others back at the beach also settled in for the night. All any of them could do was hope for rescue—or at least a drenching rain to satisfy their thirst—while keeping an eye out for Komodo dragons, snakes, and any other dangerous creatures.

11    Just as they all hoped, rescue boats were out searching for them. One person involved in the effort was Frank Winkler, who ran his own local diving business. Winkler knew all about the currents and tides of the area, and he calculated the most likely place to find the lost divers. On the morning of June 7, searchers went to the island and found Allin, Mitchinson, Pinel, and Neradairen on the beach. After picking them up, the rescue boat circled the island and found Manning. Aside from cuts, bruises, and severe lack of water, all five of the stranded companions were unharmed, and their miserable 45-hour ordeal was finally over. ✳

*If you have been timed while reading this article, enter your reading time below. Then turn to the Words-per-Minute Table on page 55 and look up your reading speed (words per minute). Enter your reading speed on the graph on page 56.*

**Reading Time: Lesson 4**

_____ : _____

*Minutes*          *Seconds*

## A Finding the Main Idea

One statement below expresses the main idea of the article. One statement is too general, or too broad. The other statement explains only part of the article; it is too narrow. Label the statements using the following key:

**M—Main Idea**　　　**B—Too Broad**　　　**N—Too Narrow**

_____ 1. A group of stranded scuba divers were threatened by a Komodo dragon.

_____ 2. The waters near Indonesia's coral reefs can be dangerous because of their strong currents.

_____ 3. A group of scuba divers was stranded for 45 hours while diving near Indonesia's coral reefs.

_____ Score 15 points for a correct M answer.

_____ Score 5 points for each correct B or N answer.

_____ **Total Score**: Finding the Main Idea

## B Recalling Facts

How well do you remember the facts in the article? Put an X in the box next to the answer that correctly completes each statement about the article.

1. The waters near Indonesia's coral reefs are located between the Pacific and
   ☐ a. Atlantic oceans.
   ☐ b. Southern oceans.
   ☐ c. Indian oceans.

2. The diver that made it to the island first was
   ☐ a. Kathleen Mitchinson.
   ☐ b. James Manning.
   ☐ c. Charlotte Allin.

3. The scuba divers on the beach tried to start a fire by
   ☐ a. striking all of the matches they had.
   ☐ b. rubbing together two sticks.
   ☐ c. using a magnifying glass.

4. Manning was scared most by a
   ☐ a. snake.
   ☐ b. bee colony.
   ☐ c. Komodo dragon.

5. The only food the divers ate on the island was
   ☐ a. raw mussels.
   ☐ b. coconuts.
   ☐ c. snakes.

Score 5 points for each correct answer.

_____ **Total Score**: Recalling Facts

# C Making Inferences

When you combine your own experiences and information from a text to draw a conclusion that is not directly stated in that text, you are making an inference. Below are five statements that may or may not be inferences based on information in the article. Label the statements using the following key:

**C—Correct Inference**        **F—Faulty Inference**

_____ 1. If the five scuba divers had split up, their chances of being saved would have been five times greater.

_____ 2. The Komodo dragon might have caused more harm, but it was not used to finding humans on the island.

_____ 3. The scuba divers were left stranded in the ocean on purpose.

_____ 4. This group of scuba divers all had similar skills and physical abilities.

_____ 5. The Indonesian coral reefs are so beautiful that divers are willing to face the dangerous waters that surround them.

Score 5 points for each correct answer.

_____ **Total Score**: Making Inferences

# D Using Words Precisely

Each numbered sentence below contains an underlined word or phrase from the article. Following the sentence are three definitions. One definition is closest to the meaning of the underlined word. One definition is opposite or nearly opposite. Label those two definitions using the following key. Do not label the remaining definition.

**C—Closest**        **O—Opposite or Nearly Opposite**

1. The divers were sitting on parched and deserted Rinca Island.

_____ a. wet, damp

_____ b. empty, uninhabited

_____ c. dry, waterless

2. Clad only in his wetsuit vest, shorts, and thin rubber diving boots, Manning climbed over the steep cliffs that bordered the coastline.

_____ a. cold

_____ b. uncovered

_____ c. clothed

3. The bees would have gone berserk if the branch had hit their colony.

_____ a. out of control

_____ b. reasonable, sensible

_____ c. loose, free

4. In the late afternoon, a huge Komodo dragon sauntered onto the beach.

_____ a. looked over

_____ b. strolled across

_____ c. rushed past

5. Manning discovered that swimming was more <u>perilous</u> than climbing the cliffs.

_____ a. safe, secure

_____ b. comfortable, restful

_____ c. dangerous, risky

_____ Score 3 points for each correct C answer.

_____ Score 2 points for each correct O answer.

_____ **Total Score**: Using Words Precisely

Enter the four total scores in the spaces below, and add them together to find your Reading Comprehension Score. Then record your score on the graph on page 57.

| Score | Question Type | Lesson 4 |
|---|---|---|
| _____ | Finding the Main Idea | |
| _____ | Recalling Facts | |
| _____ | Making Inferences | |
| _____ | Using Words Precisely | |
| _____ | **Reading Comprehension Score** | |

## Author's Approach

Put an X in the box next to the correct answer.

1. The main purpose of the first paragraph is to

☐ a. introduce the reader to Indonesia's coral reefs.

☐ b. make the reader curious about what happened on the third day of Allin's adventure and want to read more.

☐ c. describe Charlotte Allin.

2. From the statements below, choose the one that you believe the author would agree with.

☐ a. Scuba diving beginners should avoid the waters near Indonesia's coral reefs.

☐ b. The divers didn't need to swim to the island.

☐ c. Komodo dragons should be removed from Rinca Island.

3. What does the author imply by saying "Manning, a former commando who had served in Iraq and Afghanistan, set out to explore the island"?

☐ a. Manning was a soldier, not a scuba diver.

☐ b. Manning wanted to go off on his own and not be dragged down by those who were weaker than him.

☐ c. Manning's military training made him the best choice to take on the difficult task.

4. Judging by statements from the article "Stranded!" you can conclude that the author wants the reader to think

☐ a. the divers did not react well in this emergency.

☐ b. despite the stress, the five divers did not panic.

☐ c. the divers could have done more to get back to safety.

_____ Number of correct answers

Record your personal assessment of your work on the Critical Thinking Chart on page 58.

**CRITICAL THINKING**

# Summarizing and Paraphrasing

Put an X in the box next to the correct answer for questions 1 and 2. Follow the directions provided for question 3.

1. Choose the best one-sentence paraphrase for the following sentence from the article: "The 24-year-old British woman was dazzled by the astonishing beauty of Indonesia's coral reefs."

   ☐ a. The loveliness of Indonesia's coral reefs astonished the young woman from England.

   ☐ b. The reefs amazed the woman.

   ☐ c. The 24-year-old woman was excited to see the pretty coral reefs in Indonesia.

2. Read the statement from the article below. Then read the paraphrase of that statement. Choose the reason that best tells why the paraphrase does not say the same thing as the statement.

   Statement:    At sunrise the next morning, they awoke freezing cold.

   Paraphrase:  They woke up the next day at dawn, cold and hungry.

   ☐ a. Paraphrase says too much.

   ☐ b. Paraphrase doesn't say enough.

   ☐ c. Paraphrase doesn't agree with the statement.

3. Look for the important ideas and events in paragraph 6. Summarize the paragraph in one or two sentences.

   _____

   _____

   _____

   _____

   _____ Number of correct answers

   Record your personal assessment of your work on the Critical Thinking Chart on page 58.

# Critical Thinking

Follow the directions provided for questions 1, 3, and 5. Put an X in the box next to the correct answer for the other questions.

1. For each statement below, write O if it expresses an opinion or write F if it expresses a fact.

   _____ a. After nine hours in the water, the five scuba divers ended up on Rinca Island.

   _____ b. The divers were rescued on June 7, 2008.

   _____ c. The worst part of the experience for the divers was the lack of food and water.

2. From the article, you can predict that

   ☐ a. scuba divers will not be allowed in the waters near Indonesia's coral reefs because they are too dangerous.

   ☐ b. despite this experience, the five scuba divers will return to diving because they enjoy it.

   ☐ c. a rescue station will be set up on Rinca Island.

3. Choose from the letters below to correctly complete the following statement. Write the letters on the lines.

   In the article, _____ and _____ are alike because they both ran diving businesses.

   a. Frank Winkler

   b. Kathleen Mitchinson

   c. Charlotte Allin

4. What caused the divers to become stranded?

   ☐ a. The dive boat was turned away from the divers.

   ☐ b. A powerful current pushed the divers farther and farther away from the dive boat.

   ☐ c. The divers could see nearby islands, but they could not reach them.

5. In which paragraph did you find your information or details to answer question 3?

_____

| |
|---|
| _____ Number of correct answers |
| Record your personal assessment of your work on the Critical Thinking Chart on page 58. |

## Personal Response

Describe a time when you became lost.

_____

_____

_____

_____

_____

_____

_____

_____

## Self-Assessment

I'm proud of how I answered question _____ in _____ section because

_____

_____

_____

_____

_____

_____

_____

_____

_____

_____

CRITICAL THINKING

# Crash Landing

*After the crash landing, the passengers stood on the wings of the plane as they waited to be rescued.*

On January 15, 2009, Captain Chesley Sullenberger and his co-pilot, First Officer Jeffery Skiles, were in the cockpit of US Airways Flight 1549 when it took off from La Guardia Airport in New York. It was 3:25 P.M., and the plane was headed for Charlotte, North Carolina, carrying a five-person crew and 150 passengers. Skiles was at the controls of the narrow-body, medium-range Airbus A320, while Sullenberger studied the plane's instructions and flight charts. The jet quickly soared to about 3,000 feet and reached a flying speed of about 250 miles an hour. Suddenly Skiles noticed a large flock of Canadian geese off to the right. In the next moment, Sullenberger glanced up and saw out of the cockpit's windscreen a lot of large birds flying very close to the plane. He later told investigators his first instinct was to duck.

2      Seconds later, flight attendants reported hearing a strange thud. It was a sound they had never heard before. It quickly became evident that a large number of the geese had been sucked into the jet's two engines, knocking out the power in both of them. All this had happened by 3:27 P.M.—only two minutes after takeoff. Sullenberger told investigators that he could smell "burning birds." With the engines knocked out, he knew the plane wouldn't stay in the air very long, so the problem became how and where to land it. Sullenberger turned to Skiles and said, "My aircraft." In the well-understood language of commercial pilots,

this simply meant that Sullenberger was the captain and he wanted to take over the controls. Skiles responded, "Your aircraft" and moved out of the pilot's seat.

3      Pilots are trained on simulators to respond to emergencies, but there was no way to practice the situation that Sullenberger now faced. At first, Sullenberger later admitted, he had to get past the shock that what had happened was real. "Then I had the sudden realization that unlike every other flight I had at that point in 42 years, this one would probably not end on a runway with the aircraft undamaged. And I was OK with that, as long as I could solve the problem." With that issue settled in his mind, Sullenberger said, "I was able to force calm on myself."

4      Sullenberger and Skiles evaluated their choices. Skiles went through a checklist of procedures for restarting the engines, but nothing worked. By this time passengers could see flames coming from the left wing. Without the two engines' thrust, the plane was in danger of falling out of the sky. To prevent that, Sullenberger lowered the nose of the plane and began to fly it as if it was a glider instead of a jet plane. They radioed the Air Traffic Control Tower, "Hit birds. We've

lost thrust on both engines. We're turning back to LaGuardia." Controller Patrick Harten gave the plane emergency clearance to land on Runway 13, but by that time Sullenberger realized he would never make it back. The plane was "too slow, too low" and, in any event, there were "too many buildings, too populated an area." If the large commercial plane failed to make the

*US Airways pilot Chesley Sullenberger did not abandon the plane until he was sure everyone else had left.*

five miles back to the airport, and it crashed into the Manhattan skyscrapers instead, the resulting catastrophe would have been truly terrifying.

5    Sullenberger briefly thought about trying to bring the plane down at Teterboro Airport, across the Hudson River in New Jersey. Air traffic controllers quickly gained permission for an emergency landing at Teterboro. Again, Sullenberger rejected the idea when he realized that the airport was too far away and his plane lacked enough altitude. "We can't do it," he radioed. Then he announced a new plan: "We're gonna be in the Hudson."

6    Sullenberger figured that under the circumstances, a river landing offered the best chance for his passengers and crew to survive. He switched on the plane's intercom and told the passengers to "brace for impact." Then he lowered the aircraft's flaps, the movable parts on the wings that slow a plane down before it lands. It was extremely important to hit the water as slowly as possible to reduce the power of the impact. As Sullenberger guided the plane over the Hudson River, he came dangerously close to colliding with another plane, whose airspace Sullenberger had invaded. Then, as the plane continued its glide downward, it narrowly missed the George Washington Bridge.

7    About 90 seconds later, the belly of the 75-ton airplane struck and skidded along the surface of the Hudson River. Although Sullenberger had slowed the aircraft as much as possible, it still hit the water going about 150 miles an hour. Items from the serving area came loose and flew all over the cabin. Passenger Joe Hart compared the landing to a car crash. He said, "It threw you into the seat ahead of you." One passenger suffered two broken legs and others received cuts and bruises, but most of the injuries were superficial. Hart credited Sullenberger for making the landing as smooth as it was, saying, "He was phenomenal."

8    With the air temperature a freezing 20 degrees, the water temperature a bone-chilling 36 degrees, and with the plane slowly sinking as it drifted down the Hudson with the current, Sullenberger and his crew faced a new problem. They had to get everyone off the plane as quickly as possible to avoid hypothermia or possible drowning. Sullenberger knew a quick evacuation was essential for survival. In fact, he had chosen to ditch the jet in this particular part of the river precisely because he knew large boats would be operating nearby. The boats increased the chances for a rapid rescue. Local ferryboats from the NY Waterway and boats from the Circle Line Sightseeing Cruises responded almost immediately to the crisis. The first ferryboat arrived just four minutes after the ditching.

9    Meanwhile, as the plane began to sink, the three flight attendants urged passengers to escape the rising water by coming forward to emergency exits. Once outside the plane, some passengers stayed on an inflated slide attached to the door. Others climbed onto the wings, standing in water up to their knees. Very quickly, police and fire rescue boats arrived and began collecting the survivors. Captain Sullenberger twice waded through deep water inside the cabin, going up and down the aisle to make sure everyone had evacuated. He was the last person to leave the aircraft.

10    In the end, 38 people suffered some kind of injury or hypothermia, but not a single person died. National Transportation Safety Board Chairperson Deborah A. P. Hersman praised everyone involved. "Once the birds and the airplane collided and the accident became inevitable, so many things went right," she said. Captain Sullenberger made sure of that. ✳

*If you have been timed while reading this article, enter your reading time below. Then turn to the Words-per-Minute Table on page 55 and look up your reading speed (words per minute). Enter your reading speed on the graph on page 56.*

**Reading Time: Lesson 5**

_____ : _____
*Minutes*          *Seconds*

## A Finding the Main Idea

One statement below expresses the main idea of the article. One statement is too general, or too broad. The other statement explains only part of the article; it is too narrow. Label the statements using the following key:

**M—Main Idea**     **B—Too Broad**     **N—Too Narrow**

_____  1.  After two engines of US Airways Flight 1549 were damaged in a collision with geese, Captain Sullenberger was able to land the plane safely in the Hudson River.

_____  2.  A plane that has two damaged engines cannot stay in the air very long.

_____  3.  After his plane was damaged in a collision with geese, Captain Sullenberger decided to land it in the Hudson River.

_____  Score 15 points for a correct M answer.

_____  Score 5 points for each correct B or N answer.

_____  **Total Score**: Finding the Main Idea

## B Recalling Facts

How well do you remember the facts in the article? Put an X in the box next to the answer that correctly completes each statement about the article.

1.  US Airways Flight 1549 took off from an airport in
    ☐  a.  New Jersey.
    ☐  b.  North Carolina.
    ☐  c.  New York.

2.  Sullenberger decided not to fly over Manhattan to return to LaGuardia Airport because
    ☐  a.  there were too many planes in the area.
    ☐  b.  there was no airport nearby.
    ☐  c.  he was concerned about crashing into skyscrapers.

3.  Sullenberger could not land at Teterboro Airport because
    ☐  a.  the airport was too far away.
    ☐  b.  he did not gain permission for an emergency landing.
    ☐  c.  he could not get in touch with the airport's air traffic controllers.

4.  The first to arrive when the plane landed in the Hudson River was
    ☐  a.  a fire rescue boat.
    ☐  b.  a ferryboat.
    ☐  c.  a cruise ship.

5.  The last person to leave the plane was
    ☐  a.  the passenger with two broken legs.
    ☐  b.  Captain Sullenberger.
    ☐  c.  First Officer Skiles.

Score 5 points for each correct answer.

_____  **Total Score**: Recalling Facts

## C Making Inferences

When you combine your own experiences and information from a text to draw a conclusion that is not directly stated in that text, you are making an inference. Below are five statements that may or may not be inferences based on information in the article. Label the statements using the following key:

**C—Correct Inference**          **F—Faulty Inference**

_____ 1. Captain Sullenberger usually accepts responsibility quickly and completely.

_____ 2. The co-pilot should have been able to avoid colliding with the geese.

_____ 3. Collisions with large birds such as geese may have caused aircrafts to crash at other times and at other airports.

_____ 4. The air traffic controllers were frustrated with Captain Sullenberger because he kept changing his plan for landing the plane.

_____ 5. The local ferryboats and sightseeing boats reacted quickly because they have often helped other, smaller planes that crash-landed in the Hudson River.

---

Score 5 points for each correct answer.

_____ **Total Score**: Making Inferences

---

## D Using Words Precisely

Each numbered sentence below contains an underlined word or phrase from the article. Following the sentence are three definitions. One definition is closest to the meaning of the underlined word. One definition is opposite or nearly opposite. Label those two definitions using the following key. Do not label the remaining definition.

**C—Closest**          **O—Opposite or Nearly Opposite**

1. It quickly became <u>evident</u> that a large number of geese had been sucked into the jet's two engines.

_____ a. hidden, secret

_____ b. a fear, a concern

_____ c. apparent, obvious

2. Sullenberger and Skiles <u>evaluated</u> their choices.

_____ a. judged, examined

_____ b. dismissed

_____ c. called out

3. They had to get everyone off the plane as quickly as possible to avoid <u>hypothermia</u> or possible drowning.

_____ a. overheating

_____ b. lower than normal body temperature

_____ c. head injury

4. Sullenberger knew a quick <u>evacuation</u> was essential for survival.

_____ a. learning about something

_____ b. act of leaving or removing

_____ c. staying or keeping

5. Once the birds and the plane collided, the accident became <u>inevitable</u>.

_____ a. preventable, escapable

_____ b. planned, organized

_____ c. certain, unable to be avoided

_____ Score 3 points for each correct C answer.

_____ Score 2 points for each correct O answer.

_____ **Total Score**: Using Words Precisely

Enter the four total scores in the spaces below, and add them together to find your Reading Comprehension Score. Then record your score on the graph on page 57.

| Score | Question Type | Lesson 5 |
|---|---|---|
| _____ | Finding the Main Idea | |
| _____ | Recalling Facts | |
| _____ | Making Inferences | |
| _____ | Using Words Precisely | |
| _____ | **Reading Comprehension Score** | |

## Author's Approach

Put an X in the box next to the correct answer.

1. The author uses the first sentence of the article to
   - ☐ a. make the reader curious.
   - ☐ b. describe Captain Sullenberger.
   - ☐ c. answer basic questions about the story, such as who, what, when, and where.

2. The author probably wrote this article in order to
   - ☐ a. make people aware of the dangers of flying.
   - ☐ b. tell the story of an amazing emergency landing.
   - ☐ c. warn people that they should expect the unexpected.

3. Judging by statements from the article "Crash Landing," you can conclude that the author wants the reader to think that Captain Sullenberger
   - ☐ a. really did not know how to handle this emergency.
   - ☐ b. was able to stay remarkably calm in an emergency.
   - ☐ c. was lucky to have landed the plane safely.

4. In this article, the sentence "Sullenberger told the passengers to 'brace for impact'" means Sullenberger told the passengers to
   - ☐ a. prepare for a crash.
   - ☐ b. get ready in case the plane should hit more birds.
   - ☐ c. watch out for objects that might become loose and fly through the plane.

_____ Number of correct answers

Record your personal assessment of your work on the Critical Thinking Chart on page 58.

# Summarizing and Paraphrasing

Put an X in the box next to the correct answer for questions 1 and 2. Follow the directions provided for question 3.

1.  Choose the best one-sentence paraphrase for the following sentence from the article: "Sullenberger knew a quick evacuation was essential to survival."

    ☐ a.  Sullenberger knew everyone had to get off the plane in order for him to survive.

    ☐ b.  Sullenberger was aware that everyone wanted to get off the plane quickly.

    ☐ c.  Sullenberger knew that their survival depended on their ability to get off the plane quickly.

2.  Read the statement from the article below. Then read the paraphrase of that statement. Choose the reason that best tells why the paraphrase does not say the same thing as the statement.

    Statement:   Seconds later, flight attendants reported hearing a strange thud.

    Paraphrase:   Within seconds, the flight attendants said they heard an odd noise and became worried.

    ☐ a.  Paraphrase says too much.

    ☐ b.  Paraphrase doesn't say enough.

    ☐ c.  Paraphrase doesn't agree with the statement.

3.  Reread paragraph 2 in the article. Below, write a summary of the paragraph in no more than 25 words.

    _____

    _____

    _____

    _____

Reread your summary and decide whether it covers the important ideas in the paragraph. Next, try to shorten the summary to 15 words or less without leaving out any essential information. Write this summary below.

_____

_____

_____

_____

_____ Number of correct answers

Record your personal assessment of your work on the Critical Thinking Chart on page 58.

# Critical Thinking

Put an X in the box next to the correct answer for questions 1, 4, and 5. Follow the directions provided for the other questions.

1.  Which of the following statements from the article is an opinion rather than a fact?

    ☐ a.  "The jet quickly soared to about 3,000 feet and reached a flying speed of about 250 miles an hour."

    ☐ b.  "He was phenomenal."

    ☐ c.  "The belly of the 75-ton airplane struck and skidded along the surface of the Hudson River."

2.  Choose from the letters below to correctly complete the following statement. Write the letters on the lines.

    In the article, _____ and _____ were alike because they worked to get the passengers off the plane safely.

    a.  flight attendants

    b.  air traffic controllers

    c.  police and fire fighters on the rescue boats

3. Reread paragraph 2. Then choose from the letters below to correctly complete the following statement. Write the letters on the lines.

According to paragraph 2, _____ because _____.

a. a large number of geese had been sucked into the engines

b. the power in the jet's two engines was knocked out

c. Skiles moved out of the pilot's seat

4. How is "Crash Landing" an example of the theme of *Survivors*?

☐ a. Everyone on the plane faced death, but all survived because of the skill of Captain Sullenberger.

☐ b. The plane's passengers were afraid they would not survive the crash.

☐ c. You risk your life every time you fly in an airplane.

5. Judging by events in the article, you can conclude that the passengers

☐ a. were unaware there was any problem.

☐ b. did not cooperate with the rescuers.

☐ c. were extremely worried and scared.

_____ Number of correct answers

Record your personal assessment of your work on the Critical Thinking Chart on page 58.

## Personal Response

I wonder why

_____

_____

_____

_____

## Self-Assessment

From reading this article, I have learned

_____

_____

_____

_____

_____

_____

_____

_____

# Compare and Contrast

Think about the articles you have read in Unit One. Choose three articles that show a clear cause and effect. Write the titles of the articles in the first column of the chart below. Use information you learned from the articles to fill in the empty boxes in the chart.

| Title | How did the problem begin? | What was the primary threat to survival? | In what way did the people involved help each other to survive? |
|---|---|---|---|
|  |  |  |  |
|  |  |  |  |
|  |  |  |  |

The problem I would be able to survive easiest is _____

because _____

_____

_____ .

# Words-per-Minute Table

## Unit One

**Directions** If you were timed while reading an article, refer to the Reading Time you recorded in the box at the end of the article. Use this words-per-minute table to determine your reading speed for that article. Then plot your reading speed on the graph on page 56.

| Lesson | Sample | 1 | 2 | 3 | 4 | 5 | |
|---|---|---|---|---|---|---|---|
| No. of Words | 1086 | 1120 | 1160 | 1137 | 1195 | 1118 | |
| 1:30 | 724 | 747 | 773 | 758 | 797 | 745 | 90 |
| 1:40 | 652 | 672 | 696 | 682 | 717 | 671 | 100 |
| 1:50 | 592 | 611 | 633 | 620 | 652 | 610 | 110 |
| 2:00 | 543 | 560 | 580 | 569 | 598 | 559 | 120 |
| 2:10 | 501 | 517 | 535 | 525 | 552 | 516 | 130 |
| 2:20 | 465 | 480 | 497 | 487 | 512 | 479 | 140 |
| 2:30 | 434 | 448 | 464 | 455 | 478 | 447 | 150 |
| 2:40 | 407 | 420 | 435 | 426 | 448 | 419 | 160 |
| 2:50 | 383 | 395 | 409 | 401 | 422 | 395 | 170 |
| 3:00 | 362 | 373 | 387 | 379 | 398 | 373 | 180 |
| 3:10 | 343 | 354 | 366 | 359 | 377 | 353 | 190 |
| 3:20 | 326 | 336 | 348 | 341 | 359 | 335 | 200 |
| 3:30 | 310 | 320 | 331 | 325 | 341 | 319 | 210 |
| 3:40 | 296 | 305 | 316 | 310 | 326 | 305 | 220 |
| 3:50 | 283 | 292 | 303 | 297 | 312 | 292 | 230 |
| 4:00 | 272 | 280 | 290 | 284 | 299 | 280 | 240 |
| 4:10 | 261 | 269 | 278 | 273 | 287 | 268 | 250 |
| 4:20 | 251 | 258 | 268 | 262 | 276 | 258 | 260 |
| 4:30 | 241 | 249 | 258 | 253 | 266 | 248 | 270 |
| 4:40 | 233 | 240 | 249 | 244 | 256 | 240 | 280 |
| 4:50 | 225 | 232 | 240 | 235 | 247 | 231 | 290 |
| 5:00 | 217 | 224 | 232 | 227 | 239 | 224 | 300 |
| 5:10 | 210 | 217 | 225 | 220 | 231 | 216 | 310 |
| 5:20 | 204 | 210 | 218 | 213 | 224 | 210 | 320 |
| 5:30 | 197 | 204 | 211 | 207 | 217 | 203 | 330 |
| 5:40 | 192 | 198 | 205 | 201 | 211 | 197 | 340 |
| 5:50 | 186 | 192 | 199 | 195 | 205 | 192 | 350 |
| 6:00 | 181 | 187 | 193 | 190 | 199 | 186 | 360 |
| 6:10 | 176 | 182 | 188 | 184 | 194 | 181 | 370 |
| 6:20 | 171 | 177 | 183 | 180 | 189 | 177 | 380 |
| 6:30 | 167 | 172 | 178 | 175 | 184 | 172 | 390 |
| 6:40 | 163 | 168 | 174 | 171 | 179 | 168 | 400 |
| 6:50 | 159 | 164 | 170 | 166 | 175 | 164 | 410 |
| 7:00 | 155 | 160 | 166 | 162 | 171 | 160 | 420 |
| 7:10 | 152 | 156 | 162 | 159 | 167 | 156 | 430 |
| 7:20 | 148 | 153 | 158 | 155 | 163 | 152 | 440 |
| 7:30 | 145 | 149 | 155 | 152 | 159 | 149 | 450 |
| 7:40 | 142 | 146 | 151 | 148 | 156 | 146 | 460 |
| 7:50 | 139 | 143 | 148 | 145 | 153 | 143 | 470 |
| 8:00 | 136 | 140 | 145 | 142 | 149 | 140 | 480 |

*Minutes and Seconds*

*Seconds*

# Plotting Your Progress: Reading Speed

## Unit One

**Directions** If you were timed while reading an article, write your words-per-minute rate for that article in the box under the number of the lesson. Then plot your reading speed on the graph by putting a small X on the line directly above the number of the lesson, across from the number of words per minute you read. As you mark your speed for each lesson, graph your progress by drawing a line to connect the Xs.

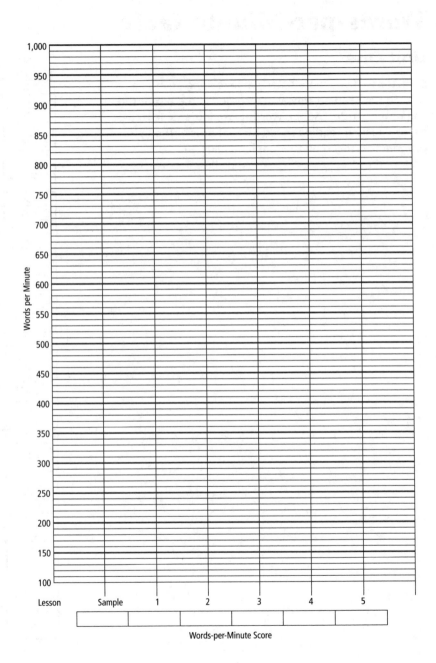

Words per Minute

Lesson    Sample    1    2    3    4    5

Words-per-Minute Score

# Plotting Your Progress: Reading Comprehension

## Unit One

**Directions** Write your Reading Comprehension score for each lesson in the box under the number of the lesson. Then plot your score on the graph by putting a small X on the line directly above the number of the lesson and across from the score you earned. As you mark your score for each lesson, graph your progress by drawing a line to connect the Xs.

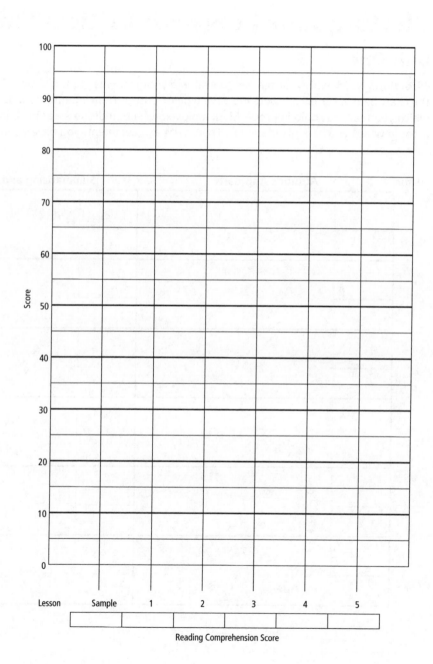

# Plotting Your Progress: Critical Thinking

## Unit One

**Directions** Work with your teacher to evaluate your responses to the Critical Thinking questions for each lesson. Then fill in the appropriate spaces in the chart below. For each lesson and each type of Critical Thinking question, do the following: Mark a minus sign (–) in the box to indicate areas in which you feel you could improve. Mark a plus sign (+) to indicate areas in which you feel you did well. Mark a minus-slash-plus sign (–/+) to indicate areas in which you had mixed success. Then write any comments you have about your performance, including ideas for improvement.

| Lesson | Author's Approach | | Summarizing and Paraphrasing | | Critical Thinking | |
|---|---|---|---|---|---|---|
| Sample | | | | | | |
| 1 | | | | | | |
| 2 | | | | | | |
| 3 | | | | | | |
| 4 | | | | | | |
| 5 | | | | | | |

# Wangjialing Mining Disaster

*The Wangjialing coal mine in northern China suddenly filled with water, trapping more than half of the working miners.*

On Sunday afternoon, March 28, 2010, 261 miners were digging tunnels in the Wangjialing coal mine in northern China when a group of them broke a wall of a nearby mining shaft that was no longer being used. As the wall broke, millions of gallons of frigid black water gushed out and flooded the narrow tunnels of the mine. It was as if an underground tidal wave was suddenly let loose. One hundred eight of the miners were close enough to the mine entrance to scramble out to safety. Many who were not so lucky drowned as the rushing water tumbled them through the winding passages. The remaining 153 miners were trapped in the rapidly filling tunnels more than 800 feet below the surface of the Earth.

2    As soon as the disaster was reported, the government launched a massive rescue effort to save the victims. About three thousand rescuers, most of them also miners, assembled outside of the Wangjialing mine and began setting up equipment. They installed 14 pumps to siphon the water out of the mine and drilled holes into the mine to pump in oxygen.

3    When the news was released to the public, thousands of loved ones and concerned citizens gathered outside of the disaster area. At first, government officials guaranteed the men would be rescued, but after four days and no signs of life, the message was toned down to simple words of hope. "It is believed that some workers may have a chance of survival," they said. Many experts who were familiar with China's

mining industry were even less certain. That is because China has one of the worst records for mining disasters in the world. Thousands of coal miners die in accidents every year in China. An accident similar to the Wangjialing flooded mine occurred in August 2007, in which a coal mine flooded in eastern Shandong province, killing 172 workers.

4    Meanwhile, down in the mine, the water level was going down little by little, thanks to the pumps. The trapped workers did what they could to help themselves survive until rescue teams could get to them. When the water poured through the breach in the wall, several miners managed to climb onto high work platforms. A few were able to grab onto wooden beams that secured the walls of the mine. From their perch on the wall, the men ripped parts of their clothing into strips and then tied themselves to the beams. Nine miners dangled there for three days until, luckily, they saw two mining carts float by. The men jumped into the carts and drifted through the winding passageways until they reached an island of dry ground.

5    After several days, all of the trapped miners were weak from lack of food. Some began to eat the bark off the pine support beams. Others ate sawdust or the paper used to wrap explosives. Some even pulled apart and ate their clothes. Most of them refused at first to drink the filthy water that had filled the mine because they feared it

*Many miners were trapped with no news for eight days and nights.*

would make them sick, but thirst forced them to drink. Some of the older miners tried to cheer up the younger, less experienced, men by telling stories of miners who had survived even worse conditions. Some older miners huddled tightly around the younger ones to provide a sense of safety and to keep them warm.

6      Back on the surface, rescuers continued to pump water out and flow oxygen and clean water in through the hollow drill pipes. After four long days, however, there was no sign of life from below, and the rescuers began to lose hope. Then, on Friday, April 2, rescue workers thought they heard sounds of tapping from below on one of the drill pipes. The workers responded by banging on the pipe with a piece of metal. After a long moment, a distant series of clangs was repeated from the depths. The excited rescuers pulled the pipe back up to the surface and found a piece of wire tied to the end. These were the first signs of life from the mine in the six days since the disaster struck.

7      The jubilant rescuers gathered and delivered hundreds of small bags of food down through the drill pipe. They also sent pens and paper and even a special phone that could be used in mines. They hoped that the miners would convey some information about their condition. After waiting for some time, nothing more was heard from below. The rescuers shouted into the pipe and banged on it some more. They sent written messages, too. One message read, "Dear brothers, please wait in patience. . . . The water will be soon drained. You must hold on and on! How about the gas and ventilation underground? What do you need us to do? Please tell us. . . ." But there was no response. The mine had gone silent.

8      In fact, the gas was precisely the reason why the miners had stopped banging on the pipes. Coal seams emit dangerous methane gas fumes, and the miners felt they could not risk any further tapping on the metal pipe. Striking metal against metal might cause a spark that would ignite an explosion from the methane gas.

9      On Saturday, April 3, rescuers thought they had pumped out enough water to go into the mine and look for the survivors. Divers were sent down into the black, murky water, but they came back within a couple of hours. The darkness, combined with the narrow maze of tunnels and the amount of water still in the mine, made finding anyone too difficult.

10      Finally, just after midnight on April 5—eight unbearable days after the mine flooded—rescue teams went back into the mine. This time, as they paddled through the low, dark passages on rubber rafts, they spotted swaying headlamps up ahead. "We first saw some lights in the distance," team leader Chen Yongsheng told reporters. "Then we realized that there were more than 100 miners there."

11      Throughout that day, the miners were brought to the entrance on the rafts and carried up to the mouth of the mine. Once there, they were wrapped in blankets and strapped onto stretchers. Before they were brought out into the open, the survivors' eyes were covered with towels to shield them from the sunlight. As each one was carried through the entrance of the mine, the thousands of loved ones and well-wishers who had been keeping vigil cheered and shouted. One hundred fifteen miners made it out of the mine alive. Most were suffering from some combination of extreme cold, thirst, low blood pressure, and skin infections from prolonged exposure to the water. Although 38 miners had perished as they waited for rescue, the number of survivors was more than anyone had a right to expect. As one coal mine safety adviser said, "This is probably one of the most amazing rescues in the history of mining anywhere." ✳

*If you have been timed while reading this article, enter your reading time below. Then turn to the Words-per-Minute Table on page 101 and look up your reading speed (words per minute). Enter your reading speed on the graph on page 102.*

**Reading Time: Lesson 6**

_____ : _____
*Minutes*         *Seconds*

## A Finding the Main Idea

One statement below expresses the main idea of the article. One statement is too general, or too broad. The other statement explains only part of the article; it is too narrow. Label the statements using the following key:

**M—Main Idea**  **B—Too Broad**  **N—Too Narrow**

_____ 1. Older miners caught in a flooded mine in China comforted and encouraged the younger workers.

_____ 2. Coal mining is surely one of the most dangerous jobs anyone could do.

_____ 3. Miners caught in a flooded mine in northern China were rescued after eight days.

_____ Score 15 points for a correct M answer.

_____ Score 5 points for each correct B or N answer.

_____ **Total Score:** Finding the Main Idea

## B Recalling Facts

How well do you remember the facts in the article? Put an X in the box next to the answer that correctly completes each statement about the article.

1. The water that flooded the Wangjialing mine came from a
   ☐ a. nearby lake.
   ☐ b. nearby mine shaft that was no longer used.
   ☐ c. broken water pipe.

2. The flood trapped
   ☐ a. 261 miners.
   ☐ b. 108 miners.
   ☐ c. 153 miners.

3. To help the trapped miners, people on the surface
   ☐ a. sent down gas masks.
   ☐ b. built an enormous shaft for miners to crawl through.
   ☐ c. installed pumps to reduce the water level.

4. The first sign that miners were still alive was the sound of
   ☐ a. tapping on a pipe.
   ☐ b. someone singing in the mine.
   ☐ c. a pickaxe scraping against a mine wall.

5. Rescuers were able to locate the survivors after they
   ☐ a. spotted lights from the miners' headlamps.
   ☐ b. heard voices deep in the mine.
   ☐ c. received GPS signals from the miners' cell phones.

Score 5 points for each correct answer.

_____ **Total Score:** Recalling Facts

## C | Making Inferences

When you combine your own experiences and information from a text to draw a conclusion that is not directly stated in that text, you are making an inference. Below are five statements that may or may not be inferences based on information in the article. Label the statements using the following key:

**C—Correct Inference**          **F—Faulty Inference**

_____ 1. None of the trapped miners had heard about the past mining disasters in China.

_____ 2. Many miners feel a brotherhood with one another and are willing to help each other in times of crisis.

_____ 3. The older, experienced miners had much less chance of surviving than the young ones did.

_____ 4. The water was dark because it contained a large amount of coal particles.

_____ 5. The last time the rescuers went into the mine, they expected to find all of the miners alive.

Score 5 points for each correct answer.

_____ **Total Score**: Making Inferences

## D | Using Words Precisely

Each numbered sentence below contains an underlined word or phrase from the article. Following the sentence are three definitions. One definition is closest to the meaning of the underlined word. One definition is opposite or nearly opposite. Label those two definitions using the following key. Do not label the remaining definition.

**C—Closest**          **O—Opposite or Nearly Opposite**

1. Millions of gallons of <u>frigid</u> black water gushed out and flooded the narrow tunnels of the mine.

_____ a. dangerous

_____ b. very hot

_____ c. extremely cold

2. When the water poured through the <u>breach</u> in the wall, several miners managed to climb onto high work platforms.

_____ a. crack or broken part

_____ b. lowest point

_____ c. solid surface

3. They hoped that the miners would <u>convey</u> some information about their condition.

_____ a. leave behind

_____ b. carry or send along

_____ c. think about

4. The <u>jubilant</u> rescuers gathered and sent down hundreds of small bags of food through the drill pipe.

_____ a. sorrowful

_____ b. curious

_____ c. joyful

5. Coal seams <u>emit</u> dangerous methane gas fumes, and the miners felt they could not risk any further tapping on the metal pipe.

_____ a. hide

_____ b. release, send out

_____ c. take in

_____ Score 3 points for each correct C answer.

_____ Score 2 points for each correct O answer.

_____ **Total Score**: Using Words Precisely

Enter the four total scores in the spaces below, and add them together to find your Reading Comprehension Score. Then record your score on the graph on page 103.

| Score | Question Type | Lesson 6 |
|---|---|---|
| _____ | Finding the Main Idea | |
| _____ | Recalling Facts | |
| _____ | Making Inferences | |
| _____ | Using Words Precisely | |
| _____ | **Reading Comprehension Score** | |

# Author's Approach

Put an X in the box next to the correct answer.

1. The author uses the first sentence of the article to
   □ a. tell exactly where the Wangjialing mine is.
   □ b. describe the setting of the action and the problem the coal miners faced.
   □ c. point out that a group of miners were working together when the problem started.

2. What is the author's purpose in writing this article?
   □ a. to compare mine safety in China and the United States
   □ b. to describe the health problems of miners
   □ c. to entertain with an exciting story of survival

3. The author tells this story mainly by
   □ a. describing events in the order they happened.
   □ b. comparing different topics.
   □ c. using imagination or creativity.

4. Which of the following statements from the article best describes the Wangjialing miners' chances of survival?
   □ a. "When the news was released to the public, thousands of loved ones and concerned citizens gathered outside of the disaster area."
   □ b. "Thousands of coal miners die in accidents every year in China."
   □ c. "At first, government officials guaranteed the men would be rescued, but after four days and no signs of life, the message was toned down to simple words of hope."

_____ Number of correct answers

Record your personal assessment of your work on the Critical Thinking Chart on page 104.

**CRITICAL THINKING**

# Summarizing and Paraphrasing

Follow the directions provided for questions 1 and 2. Put an X in the box next to the correct answer for question 3.

1. Complete the following one-sentence summary of the article using the lettered phrases from the phrase bank below. Write the letters on the lines.

---

**Phrase Bank:**

a. the exit of the rescued miners from the mine

b. the miners' efforts to survive and the rescuers' efforts to save them

c. the flooding of the mine tunnels

---

The article "Wangjialing Mining Disaster" begins with _____, goes on to describe _____, and ends with _____.

2. Look for the important ideas and events in paragraphs 4 and 5. Summarize those paragraphs in one or two sentences.

_____

_____

_____

_____

_____

_____

_____

_____

_____

3. Choose the sentence that correctly restates the following sentence from the article: "The darkness, combined with the narrow maze of tunnels and the amount of water still in the mine, made finding anyone too difficult."

☐ a. Because the tunnels were still filled with water, rescuers could not locate any survivors.

☐ b. It was hard to find anyone because the narrow, winding tunnels were so dark and filled with water.

☐ c. The dark, watery tunnels made finding survivors very difficult.

---

_____ Number of correct answers

Record your personal assessment of your work on the Critical Thinking Chart on page 104.

---

# Critical Thinking

Follow the directions provided for questions 1 and 2. Put an X in the box next to the correct answer for the other questions.

1. For each statement below, write O if it expresses an opinion or write F if it expresses a fact.

_____ a. About three thousand rescuers, many of them also miners, began working around the clock.

_____ b. Thousands of coal miners die in accidents every year in China.

_____ c. "This is probably one of the most amazing rescues in the history of mining anywhere."

2. Reread paragraph 11. Then choose from the letters below to correctly complete the following statement. Write the letters on the lines.

According to paragraph 11, _____ because _____.

a. some rescued miners spent so long in the flood waters

b. some rescued miners suffered from skin infections

c. rescuers covered some miners' eyes with towels

3. How is "Wangjialing Mining Disaster" an example of the theme of *Survivors*?

☐ a. Many miners survived in spite of life-threatening conditions.

☐ b. Rescuers almost gave up hope of the miners' survival.

☐ c. The Wangjialing mine flood was a terrible disaster.

4. From the information in paragraph 7, you can conclude that

☐ a. the food the rescuers sent down never reached the miners.

☐ b. the miners did not read the messages the rescuers sent.

☐ c. the phone that the miners had been given could not send calls to the surface.

5. What did you have to do to answer question 2?

☐ a. find a cause (why something happened)

☐ b. find an opinion (what someone thinks about something)

☐ c. find a comparison (how things are the same)

_____ Number of correct answers

Record your personal assessment of your work on the Critical Thinking Chart on page 104.

## Personal Response

Would you recommend this article to other students? Why or why not?

_____

_____

_____

_____

## Self-Assessment

What concepts or ideas from the article were difficult to understand?

_____

_____

_____

Which were easy to understand?

_____

_____

_____

_____

# Shelter from the Storm

*The Dominguez family took shelter in a drainage pipe beneath a bridge after becoming lost in a blizzard.*

It sounded like a fun adventure: The family wanted to go out into the woods to cut down the perfect Christmas tree. So Frederick Dominguez and his three children set out from their home in northern California and drove into the wooded mountains. It was a clear, snowless Sunday afternoon on December 16, 2007. Dominguez had grown up in sunny southern California, and he had moved his family to a small mountain town northeast of Sacramento just a few months earlier. Neither he nor any of his children—Christopher, age 18, Alexis, age 15, and Joshua, age 12—thought much about snow or what might happen if they got caught in a snowstorm. None of them were properly prepared for true winter weather. Instead, they were dressed for a nice fall day, wearing just light jackets, sweatshirts, and gym shoes. They carried no food or equipment other than a saw to cut down a tree. They did not bring hats or gloves or hiking boots.

2     Dominguez parked their pickup truck off a narrow mountain road. He and the children walked from tree to tree to try and find the best one for their upcoming Christmas celebration. At last they found one they all loved, and Dominguez used the saw to cut it down. Only then did the group realize that in walking from tree to tree, they had become disoriented and

didn't know which way to go to get back to the truck. For two hours they searched without finding a familiar spot or landmark to indicate where they'd been. Then it started to grow dark and cold, and Dominguez realized they would have to spend the night in the mountains. They had cell phones with them, but in this remote area the cell phones did not work. Dominguez and his children used the light from the phones to guide them as they constructed a temporary shelter from twigs and tree branches. In the middle of the night it started snowing hard, so Dominguez and Christopher used their bodies to shield the two younger children from the biting winds and blowing snow. Neither Dominguez nor Christopher got any sleep that first night.

3    In the morning, the family stared up at a swirling blizzard. Eight inches of snow had already fallen overnight, and more kept coming down. If they were going to survive, the family needed to either make their way back to the truck or find a better place for shelter. "I just remember walking and walking and thinking, 'We're not going to make it.' I remember being really, really scared," said Alexis later.

4    Luckily, they stumbled onto an old dirt road that had a culvert, or drainage tunnel, running underneath it. The culvert was put in to allow a creek to flow under the road. The family discovered the mouth of the culvert below a small bridge and they scrambled down the bank to look inside. It was cold and wet in there—a miserable place to spend a night—but it was much better than any shelter they could build from branches. As they huddled inside it, Dominguez tried everything he could think of to lift his children's spirits. They passed the long hours singing favorite songs, telling jokes, and sharing fantasies about restaurants where they liked to eat. "The only food we had was in our thoughts,"

Dominguez quipped. At one point, when he saw Joshua becoming despondent, Dominguez said to him, "Son, I would tell you what I bought you for Christmas if I thought we weren't going to make it." Although Dominguez tried to sound easy and confident, he later admitted, "My kids were relying on me, and I was scared, but you can't tell them you're scared."

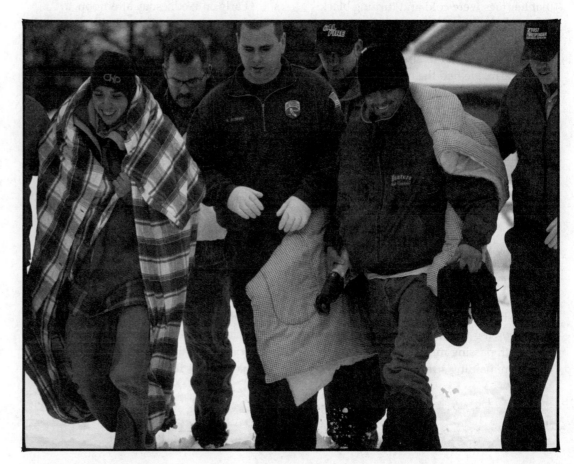

*Rescuers in helicopters located the lost family just before another snowstorm was due to arrive.*

5     Cold, wet, tired, and hopelessly lost, all he and his children could do was hope and pray that they would be rescued. Without food or proper clothing, however, time was running short. As the snow slowly melted, it dripped and drained down into and through the culvert in which the family was huddling. Alexis had lost one of her shoes, and by Tuesday, she began complaining that her toes were cold and turning black. Dominguez took off his sweatshirt, ripped it into strips, and wrapped the pieces around Alexis's feet in an attempt to keep them warm. He had the other children tuck their feet inside one another's shirts to ward off severe frostbite.

6     Meanwhile, Lisa Sams, the children's mother and Dominguez's ex-wife, reported her children missing when they did not show up at school on Monday. Hundreds of search-and-rescue officials from Nevada and California mobilized and began scouring the steep hills and canyons. Unfortunately, the heavy snow and fierce winds created drifts as high as seven feet, which made tracking the family extremely difficult.

7     By Wednesday morning, the Dominguez family still had not been found, and they were growing weaker and more fearful with each passing minute. They used most of their remaining strength to stamp the word "HELP" in the snow and fill in the letters with twigs and branches. Up to this point, searching by air had not been feasible because of the heavy cloud cover. But on Wednesday the rescuers finally got a break in the weather, and the skies cleared for a few hours. The rescuers knew they had to act fast, though, because another big storm was expected to move in.

8     Early on Wednesday afternoon, a California Highway Patrol helicopter piloted by Steve Ward flew over the search area. Ward and paramedic David White strained to see movement in the wilderness below, or at least some sign of humans—a shirt tied to a branch, tracks, or a burned out campfire. They were about to call it a day when they suddenly spotted a man frantically waving his arms up at them. At first, White and Ward thought it might be one of the searchers, but when they saw the letters "HELP" written in the snow, they realized they had found the lost family.

9     "This was our last pass," Ward said. "We were very lucky that we saw this guy."

10     It was Alexis who first had heard the helicopter overhead. Dominguez ran barefoot through several feet of snow to wave it down. Ward landed the helicopter in two feet of snow in a spot that turned out to be just a couple of miles from Frederick Dominguez's parked pickup truck. Ward and White rescued Alexis and Joshua first and then returned to pick up Christopher and his father. Doctors at the Feather River Hospital treated the four survivors for frostbite and hypothermia, saying all would make complete recoveries. "I'm surprised how good they are," said Doctor Kurt Bower.

11     Frederick Dominguez was grateful to have survived—and he had certainly learned his lesson about winter weather in northern California. "Next time I go out there, I won't be a knucklehead," he said. "I'll have some boots on." ✸

---

*If you have been timed while reading this article, enter your reading time below. Then turn to the Words-per-Minute Table on page 101 and look up your reading speed (words per minute). Enter your reading speed on the graph on page 102.*

**Reading Time: Lesson 7**

_____ : _____
*Minutes*      *Seconds*

## A Finding the Main Idea

One statement below expresses the main idea of the article. One statement is too general, or too broad. The other statement explains only part of the article; it is too narrow. Label the statements using the following key:

**M—Main Idea**　　**B—Too Broad**　　**N—Too Narrow**

_____　1.　A week before Christmas in 2007, the Dominguez family went out to cut down the perfect Christmas tree.

_____　2.　Frederick Dominguez was not used to winter weather.

_____　3.　The Dominguez family became lost for days in a winter storm in the California woods while looking for a Christmas tree.

_____　Score 15 points for a correct M answer.

_____　Score 5 points for each correct B or N answer.

_____　**Total Score**: Finding the Main Idea

## B Recalling Facts

How well do you remember the facts in the article? Put an X in the box next to the answer that correctly completes each statement about the article.

1.　The only equipment that the Dominguez family brought with them was
　☐　a.　an axe.
　☐　b.　a hatchet.
　☐　c.　a saw.

2.　When the family made a shelter, they used the light from
　☐　a.　their cell phones.
　☐　b.　flashlights.
　☐　c.　lanterns.

3.　The child whose toes were turning black was
　☐　a.　Christopher.
　☐　b.　Alexis.
　☐　c.　Joshua.

4.　To attract the attention of rescuers, the Dominguez family
　☐　a.　tried to start a fire.
　☐　b.　built a tower of twigs and branches.
　☐　c.　stamped the word "HELP" in the snow.

5.　The Dominguez's pickup truck was
　☐　a.　only 100 feet away from where they camped.
　☐　b.　a couple of miles away from where they camped.
　☐　c.　on the other side of the mountain from where they camped.

Score 5 points for each correct answer.

_____　**Total Score**: Recalling Facts

## C Making Inferences

When you combine your own experiences and information from a text to draw a conclusion that is not directly stated in that text, you are making an inference. Below are five statements that may or may not be inferences based on information in the article. Label the statements using the following key:

**C—Correct Inference**          **F—Faulty Inference**

_____ 1. If there had been snow on the ground they probably would have been able to find their way back to their truck.

_____ 2. The family probably wandered in many directions as they looked at trees to cut.

_____ 3. It is very unusual for so much snow to fall in the mountains of northern California.

_____ 4. Frederick Dominguez strongly believed that thinking positive thoughts was important to their survival.

_____ 5. Lisa Sams was more angry than concerned when she learned that the children had not shown up for school.

---

Score 5 points for each correct answer.

_____ **Total Score**: Making Inferences

---

## D Using Words Precisely

Each numbered sentence below contains an underlined word or phrase from the article. Following the sentence are three definitions. One definition is closest to the meaning of the underlined word. One definition is opposite or nearly opposite. Label those two definitions using the following key. Do not label the remaining definition.

**C—Closest**          **O—Opposite or Nearly Opposite**

1. They had become disoriented and didn't know which way to go to get back to the truck.

_____ a. aware

_____ b. made sick

_____ c. confused, unsure

2. The family had cell phones with them, but in this remote area the cell phones didn't work.

_____ a. distant, out-of-the-way

_____ b. close, nearby

_____ c. strange, unfamiliar

3. At one point during the night they spent in the culvert, Dominguez saw Joshua becoming despondent.

_____ a. frightened

_____ b. hopeless

_____ c. cheerful

4. The rescuers mobilized and began searching the hills and canyons.

_____ a. scattered without a plan

_____ b. assembled and prepared

_____ c. listened

5. Searching by air had not been <u>feasible</u> because of the thick clouds.

_____ a.   possible or realistic

_____ b.   not very likely

_____ c.   permitted

---

_____ Score 3 points for each correct C answer.

_____ Score 2 points for each correct O answer.

_____ **Total Score**: Using Words Precisely

---

Enter the four total scores in the spaces below, and add them together to find your Reading Comprehension Score. Then record your score on the graph on page 103.

| Score | Question Type | Lesson 7 |
|---|---|---|
| _____ | Finding the Main Idea | |
| _____ | Recalling Facts | |
| _____ | Making Inferences | |
| _____ | Using Words Precisely | |
| _____ | **Reading Comprehension Score** | |

## Author's Approach

Put an X in the box next to the correct answer.

1. The author uses the first sentence of the article to
   - ☐ a.   explain a common way for people to obtain Christmas trees.
   - ☐ b.   introduce a story about a family gathering for Christmas.
   - ☐ c.   set up a contrast with what happened after they had found and cut down the Christmas tree.

2. The author tells this story mainly by
   - ☐ a.   describing the events from the father's point of view.
   - ☐ b.   comparing the memories of each family member.
   - ☐ c.   telling the events in the order in which they happened.

3. Considering the statement from the article "Alexis had lost one of her shoes, and by Tuesday, she began complaining that her toes were cold and turning black," you can conclude that the author wants the reader to think that
   - ☐ a.   the extreme cold and damp conditions had caused her toes to change color.
   - ☐ b.   Alexis had walked through mud.
   - ☐ c.   Alexis was too concerned about her cold toes.

4. In this article, "They were about to call it a day," means the rescuers
   - ☐ a.   were going to stop searching.
   - ☐ b.   were about to make a phone call.
   - ☐ c.   realized it was getting late.

---

_____ Number of correct answers

Record your personal assessment of your work on the Critical Thinking Chart on page 104.

# Summarizing and Paraphrasing

Put an X in the box next to the correct answer for questions 1 and 2. Follow the directions provided for question 3.

1. Choose the best one-sentence paraphrase for the following sentence from the article: "Dominguez tried everything he could think of to lift his children's spirits."

☐ a. Dominguez tried hard to give his children hope.

☐ b. Dominguez did a number of things to protect his children.

☐ c. Despite his best efforts, Dominguez was not able to put his children in a good mood.

2. Below are summaries of the article. Choose the summary that says all the most important things about the article but in the fewest words.

☐ a. Dominguez and his children were lost for three days because they could not find their truck. Rescuers in a helicopter finally found them.

☐ b. Lost in the woods, Dominguez and his children made a shelter out of twigs. Then they found shelter in a culvert. Dominguez tried to keep his children's spirits up. They were rescued after three days.

☐ c. Dominguez and his three children went out to cut down a Christmas tree. They became lost and spent three cold, miserable days in the woods before they were rescued.

3. Reread the first paragraph in the article. Below, write a summary of the paragraph in no more than 25 words.

_____

_____

_____

_____

_____

_____

_____

_____

---

_____ Number of correct answers

Record your personal assessment of your work on the Critical Thinking Chart on page 104.

---

# Critical Thinking

Follow the directions provided for questions 1 and 3. Put an X in the box next to the correct answer for the other questions.

1. For each statement below, write O if it expresses an opinion or write F if it expresses a fact.

_____ a. The Dominguez family set out to cut down a Christmas tree on December 16, 2007.

_____ b. Christopher Dominguez didn't do enough to protect his sisters and help them get a positive attitude.

_____ c. Hundreds of searchers from Nevada and California looked for the Dominguez family.

2. From the article, you can predict that if the Dominguez family goes out to cut down a Christmas tree again, they will

☐ a. bring more than just a saw to cut down the tree.

☐ b. keep better track of where they walk and not get lost.

☐ c. tell police where they are going and how long they'll be gone.

3. Choose from the letters below to correctly complete the following statement. Write the letters on the lines.

In the article, _____ and _____ are alike because they offered some protection from the snow and cold.

   a. the small bridge

   b. the culvert

   c. the makeshift shelter of twigs and branches

4. From the information in paragraph 1, you can conclude that

☐ a. Dominguez and his children were not used to snowy winter weather.

☐ b. the Dominguez children did not own winter coats.

☐ c. the Dominguez family had to drive a great distance from their home to the woods.

5. What did you have to do to answer question 3?

☐ a. find a cause (why something happened)

☐ b. find a comparison (how things are the same)

☐ c. find an effect (something that happened)

_____ Number of correct answers

Record your personal assessment of your work on the Critical Thinking Chart on page 104.

## Personal Response

What do you think was Frederick Dominguez's best decision? Why?

_____

_____

_____

_____

## Self-Assessment

From reading this article I have learned

_____

_____

_____

_____

_____

_____

_____

**CRITICAL THINKING**

# Nelson Mandela

## Never Give Up

*South Africa's civil rights leader spent 27 years as a political prisoner.*

In 1993 Nelson Mandela won the Nobel Peace Prize. One year later he became the first black man elected president of South Africa. Since then, honors and awards have been heaped upon him by leaders from around the world. As an article in *Newsweek* magazine proclaimed in 2009, "Mandela rightly occupies an untouched place in the South African imagination. He's the national liberator, the savior, its Washington and Lincoln rolled into one." Yet before any of this happened, Nelson Mandela had to survive 27 years as a political prisoner in South Africa.

2   When Mandela was a young man, South Africa was governed by apartheid, a system of legal racial segregation. Under this system, whites held all of the political power, while people who were not white were denied even the most basic human rights. Black people couldn't move about freely in their own country. All basic social services from public education to health care for blacks were vastly inferior to those offered to whites. Everything from ambulances to churches to park benches was segregated. As a leader in the fight against this discrimination, Mandela constantly ran into trouble with the law. He spoke out against these injustices and was arrested and jailed several times. Then, in

1964, the government had enough of Nelson Mandela, and they convicted him of treason and sentenced him to life in prison.

3 Mandela spent the next 18 years in prison on Robben Island, a small piece of land about five miles off the southern coast of South Africa. "Robben Island was without question the harshest, most iron-fisted outpost in the South African penal system," Mandela later wrote in his autobiography. "The warders . . . demanded a master-servant relationship. The racial divide on Robben Island was absolute: There were no black warders, and no white prisoners."

4 Prisoners on the island were ranked in one of four groups: A, B, C, or D. The "A" prisoners were common criminals, and the "D" prisoners, the political prisoners such as Mandela, were the lowest group with the fewest privileges. The "D" prisoners were allowed just one visitor and one letter every six months. Even when Mandela did get a letter, it was often unreadable because the prison censors blacked out whole paragraphs of it. When Mandela's mother died, and later when his eldest son was killed in a car accident, Mandela asked for permission to attend the funeral services. In each case, his request was denied.

5 Life inside the prison was one of endless misery and denial. Warders routinely screamed at the prisoners, made prisoners take off their hats whenever a warder walked by, and required prisoners to keep their khaki jackets buttoned up tight. Any disobeyed rule resulted in either solitary confinement or the loss of meals. Mandela

and the other prisoners spent their days pounding limestone rocks into powder and harvesting seaweed. When not working, he was locked in a small cell with only the floor as his bed. Prison cells had no running water, and instead of toilets inmates used small iron buckets. Once a day, after work, the prisoners were led to a bathroom to wash. The bathroom had two saltwater

showers, a saltwater sink, and three large metal buckets, which were used as bathtubs. With no hot water for washing, the prisoners had to wash in icy cold water. They often would sing as they washed to take their minds off of the freezing temperature.

6 The purpose of the physical hardship and the indignity was to break the prisoners' spirit. The prisoners knew they

*Nelson Mandela and his wife Winnie celebrate his release from prison.*

had to push back against the cruelty as much as they were able so that they could maintain their self-respect and humanity. Prisoners were not allowed to have a watch, so Mandela and the other prisoners marked time by listening for the ringing of the prison bell. Since every day was the same as the last, Mandela knew it would be easy to lose track of weeks and months, so he drew a calendar on his cell wall. "Losing a sense of time is an easy way to lose one's grip and even one's sanity," he later wrote. Keeping a sense of time was important even for a prisoner like Mandela, who was serving a life sentence. That is because Mandela never really believed that he would finish all of his time in prison. Mandela's friend and fellow prisoner at Robben Island for 10 years, Fikile Bam, explained, "You see, we couldn't afford to think of a life sentence in real terms, that it meant just what it said. It was, in fact, a condition of our survival in prison to believe that we would win. The struggle would be successful in the end. We'd be out of prison during our lifetime." He added, "Nelson actually lived that belief more than anyone else I knew."

7    Over the years, the warders came to respect Mandela for his intelligence, dignity, and charm. Even though their roles were far from equal, Mandela was not afraid to speak his mind to the warders.

When Mandela became angry, he spoke to them in a softer voice than usual, but with a firmer tone. He would tell the warders that he preferred to be treated with decency. From Mandela's point of view, he had been fighting for decency all of his life, and he wasn't going to give it up just because he had gone to prison.

8    After 18 years, Mandela was moved off of Robben Island. He was transferred first to Pollsmoor Prison, and then four years after that to Victor Verster Prison. Although he remained a political prisoner, conditions improved for him. One reason for the improvement was that a worldwide movement had been started to free him. Slowly, the rest of the world had caught up with what Mandela had always known: Apartheid was a vicious and unjust system that had no place in the civilized world. By the mid-1980s, South Africa was being pressured by democratic countries, including the United States, to renounce apartheid. A number of international companies refused to join in business deals with South Africa as long as apartheid remained in place. South African leaders offered to release Mandela, but only if he agreed not to cause any more trouble. However, Mandela firmly refused this deal with these daring words: "Only free men can negotiate; a prisoner cannot enter into contracts."

9    After several more years F. W. de Klerk became the leader of South Africa. De Klerk saw the handwriting on the wall and ended the apartheid system. On February 11, 1990, Mandela walked out of Victor Verster Prison a free man. He and de Klerk then led South Africa to adopt a new democratic constitution that eliminated all forms of official discrimination against black South Africans. In 1994 Nelson Mandela, the former prisoner, was elected president of South Africa, becoming the greatest symbol of hope for all oppressed people. ✷

---

*If you have been timed while reading this article, enter your reading time below. Then turn to the Words-per-Minute Table on page 101 and look up your reading speed (words per minute). Enter your reading speed on the graph on page 102.*

**Reading Time: Lesson 8**

_____ : _____
*Minutes*          *Seconds*

# A Finding the Main Idea

One statement below expresses the main idea of the article. One statement is too general, or too broad. The other statement explains only part of the article; it is too narrow. Label the statements using the following key:

**M—Main Idea**     **B—Too Broad**     **N—Too Narrow**

_____ 1. South Africa used to be governed by a system of racial segregation called apartheid.

_____ 2. Nelson Mandela was imprisoned for many years for fighting against discrimination, and later he was elected the first black president of South Africa.

_____ 3. Nelson Mandela, the first black president of South Africa, won many honors and awards including the Nobel Peace Prize.

_____ Score 15 points for a correct M answer.

_____ Score 5 points for each correct B or N answer.

_____ **Total Score**: Finding the Main Idea

# B Recalling Facts

How well do you remember the facts in the article? Put an X in the box next to the answer that correctly completes each statement about the article.

1. Nelson Mandela won the Nobel Peace Prize in
   - ☐ a. 1964.
   - ☐ b. 1990.
   - ☐ c. 1993.

2. Mandela was a political prisoner in South Africa for
   - ☐ a. 10 years.
   - ☐ b. 18 years.
   - ☐ c. 27 years.

3. The first of three prisons where Mandela spent time was
   - ☐ a. Victor Verster Prison.
   - ☐ b. Pollsmoor Prison.
   - ☐ c. Robben Island.

4. Mandela was denied permission to attend the funeral of
   - ☐ a. his father.
   - ☐ b. his oldest son.
   - ☐ c. his wife.

5. The leader of South Africa who ended the apartheid system was
   - ☐ a. F. W. de Klerk.
   - ☐ b. Fikile Bam.
   - ☐ c. Nelson Mandela.

Score 5 points for each correct answer.

_____ **Total Score**: Recalling Facts

## C Making Inferences

When you combine your own experiences and information from a text to draw a conclusion that is not directly stated in that text, you are making an inference. Below are five statements that may or may not be inferences based on information in the article. Label the statements using the following key:

**C—Correct Inference**          **F—Faulty Inference**

_____ 1. Nelson Mandela fought alone against discrimination in South Africa.

_____ 2. All white people in South Africa supported apartheid.

_____ 3. Nelson Mandela is considered a great man not only in South Africa but also around the world.

_____ 4. South African leaders did not want to release Mandela from prison because they were afraid he would continue his protests against the government.

_____ 5. Although Mandela and F. W. de Klerk worked together, they did not get along well.

Score 5 points for each correct answer.

_____ **Total Score**: Making Inferences

## D Using Words Precisely

Each numbered sentence below contains an underlined word or phrase from the article. Following the sentence are three definitions. One definition is closest to the meaning of the underlined word. One definition is opposite or nearly opposite. Label those two definitions using the following key. Do not label the remaining definition.

**C—Closest**          **O—Opposite or Nearly Opposite**

1. Apartheid was a system of legal racial <u>segregation</u>.

   _____ a. mixing together

   _____ b. government

   _____ c. separation, isolation

2. The purpose of the <u>indignity</u> was to break the prisoners' spirit.

   _____ a. assignment

   _____ b. feeling of respect

   _____ c. shame or disgrace

3. South Africa was being pressured by democratic countries to <u>renounce</u> apartheid.

   _____ a. accept completely

   _____ b. abandon, reject

   _____ c. vote on

4. "Only free men can <u>negotiate</u>; a prisoner cannot enter into contracts."

   _____ a. talk over and discuss terms

   _____ b. guess the outcome

   _____ c. refuse all offers

4. Nelson Mandela, the former prisoner, became the greatest symbol of hope for all <u>oppressed</u> people.

_____ a. starving

_____ b. governed unfairly

_____ c. provided equal rights

_____ Score 3 points for each correct C answer.

_____ Score 2 points for each correct O answer.

_____ **Total Score**: Using Words Precisely

Enter the four total scores in the spaces below, and add them together to find your Reading Comprehension Score. Then record your score on the graph on page 103.

| Score | Question Type | Lesson 8 |
|-------|---------------|----------|
| _____ | Finding the Main Idea | |
| _____ | Recalling Facts | |
| _____ | Making Inferences | |
| _____ | Using Words Precisely | |
| _____ | **Reading Comprehension Score** | |

## Author's Approach

Put an X in the box next to the correct answer.

1. What does the author imply by the statement "Over the years, the warders came to respect Mandela for his intelligence, dignity, and charm"?

☐ a. The warders seemed mean and tough, but they really were not cruel men.

☐ b. As time passed, the guards treated the prisoners better.

☐ c. The more the warders learned about Mandela, the more they were impressed by him.

2. Which of the following statements best describes Nelson Mandela?

☐ a. On February 11, 1990, Nelson Mandela walked out of prison a free man.

☐ b. Mandela is South Africa's national liberator, the savior, its Washington and Lincoln rolled into one.

☐ c. As a leader in the fight against discrimination, Mandela constantly ran into trouble with the law.

3. Which of the following statements from the article best describes the way Mandela behaved with his warders?

☐ a. "There were no black warders, and no white prisoners."

☐ b. "When not working, he was locked in a small cell with only the floor as his bed."

☐ c. "Even though their roles were far from equal, Mandela was not afraid to speak his mind to the warders."

_____ Number of correct answers

Record your personal assessment of your work on the Critical Thinking Chart on page 104.

CRITICAL THINKING

## Summarizing and Paraphrasing

Put an X in the box next to the correct answer for question 1. Follow the directions provided for questions 2 and 3.

1. Choose the best one-sentence paraphrase for the following sentence from the article: "De Klerk saw the handwriting on the wall and ended the apartheid system."

☐ a. De Klerk read the messages sent to him by the world's governments and businesses and ended apartheid.

☐ b. De Klerk realized that the apartheid system was going to fail and chose to end it himself.

☐ c. De Klerk realized how unpopular apartheid was by the graffiti on walls, so he brought it to an end.

2. Complete the following one-sentence summary of the article using the lettered phrases from the phrase bank below. Write the letters on the lines.

> **Phrase Bank:**
> a. Mandela's work with F. W. de Klerk
> b. Mandela's life in prison
> c. a list of the honors Mandela has received

The article, "Nelson Mandela: Never Give Up" begins with _____, goes on to describe _____, and ends with _____.

3. Look for the important ideas and events in paragraphs 2 and 3. Summarize those paragraphs in one or two sentences.

_____

_____

_____

_____

> _____ Number of correct answers
>
> Record your personal assessment of your work on the Critical Thinking Chart on page 104.

## Critical Thinking

Put an X in the box next to the correct answer for questions 1, 4, and 5. Follow the directions provided for the other questions.

1. Which of the following statements from the article is an opinion rather than a fact?

☐ a. "By the mid-1980s, South Africa was being pressured by democratic countries, including the United States, to renounce apartheid."

☐ b. "In 1994 Nelson Mandela, the former prisoner, was elected president of South Africa, becoming the greatest symbol of hope for all oppressed people."

☐ c. "After several more years F. W. de Klerk became the leader of South Africa."

2. Why did Mandela refuse the prison's offer of freedom if he promised not to cause trouble?

a. Mandela did not want to make a deal with the prison that treated him so poorly.

b. Mandela could not promise to give up his fight to end apartheid.

c. Mandela no longer minded living in prison.

3. Reread paragraph 8. Then choose from the letters below to correctly complete the following statement. Write the letters on the lines.

According to paragraph 8, _____ because _____.

a. a number of companies refused to do business in South Africa

b. conditions improved for Mandela

c. a worldwide movement had been started to free him

4. How is Nelson Mandela an example of the theme of *Survivors*?

☐ a. Mandela and de Klerk worked together to adopt a new national constitution.

☐ b. Mandela spoke out against the injustices of apartheid.

☐ c. Mandela lived through many years as a political prisoner to become a respected world leader.

5. From the information in paragraph 4, you can conclude that

☐ a. prisoners were never allowed out to attend funerals.

☐ b. none of the prisoners in the "D" group ever were allowed outside of the prison.

☐ c. the "D" group was the smallest group of prisoners.

_____ Number of correct answers

Record your personal assessment of your work on the Critical Thinking Chart on page 104.

## Personal Response

What would you have done if you had lived in a country governed by apartheid?

_____

_____

_____

_____

## Self-Assessment

Which concepts or ideas from the article were difficult to understand?

_____

_____

_____

_____

Which were easy to understand?

_____

_____

_____

_____

# Rough Track

*Danelle Ballengee, one of the world's best adventure sports athletes, found trouble on an unmapped route.*

One night in Moab, Utah, a neighbor of 36-year-old Danelle Ballengee noticed that the lights remained on in Ballengee's empty house for the second day in a row. Alarmed, the neighbor called Ballengee's parents. They hadn't heard a word from their daughter. Late on Thursday, Ballengee's parents notified the police, who checked the house for signs of criminal activity and found none. The police then issued a multistate bulletin for Ballengee's missing truck. On Friday morning, Detective Craig Shumway began to check the trailheads in the nearby mountains. On a hunch, he looked beyond the usual trails to a remote one used only by locals. His hunch was right; he soon found Ballengee's truck. However, there were no other signs of the missing woman. By 1:00 P.M. on Friday, a 12-member rescue party had assembled in downtown Moab.

2    Everyone knew Danelle. She was a world-class adventure racer. In the sport of adventure racing, athletes run, hike, climb, bike, and paddle through some of the most forbidden areas of the world. Injuries ranging from blistered feet to torn knee ligaments and broken bones all are part of the sport, and Ballengee had been through these trials and more. In 2000, for example, she was competing in a race on the tropical island of Borneo when a leech attached

85

itself to her eye! Ballengee has had several dramatic triumphs: she won the Pikes Peak Marathon in Colorado four times and established a women's record by hiking up and down all of Colorado's 54 peaks. Despite all of her hard-core training and discipline, however, Ballengee was not prepared for what happened to her on Wednesday, December 13, 2006.

3   At noon on that very cold day, Ballengee headed out on an easy 10-mile jog near her home in the desert of Moab, accompanied by her dog Taz, a 3-year-old German shepherd/golden retriever mix. Ballengee wore baggy running pants, a fleece hat, and three light upper layers, including a thin fleece jacket, and she carried a water bottle and two raspberry-flavored energy gels. Looking for something more interesting than a jog along a paved road, she drove her truck up to an isolated location in the mountains. There she planned to cover part of a trail called Amasa Back, a popular route during warmer months, and then to split off onto some obscure unmapped trails known only to locals.

4   About an hour into her run, the trouble happened. Ballengee was scrambling up one of the narrow mountain trails along the edge of a high cliff. Suddenly her foot slipped, and she slid over the cliff's edge, desperately trying to grab something solid. Ballengee plunged 60 feet nearly straight down, crashing into three successive rock faces before landing at the bottom of the canyon. The horrific fall shattered her pelvis in four places and cracked it in others,

leaving the bottom half of her body nearly immobile. Ballengee could move her toes, so she knew she wasn't paralyzed, but she could not stand up. Taz, seeing Ballengee sprawled on the ground, came running down from the trail and waited there next to her.

5   Through the pain came one clear thought: she had to get out of the canyon as soon as possible or else she would freeze to death. If she couldn't walk, she would have to crawl with her hands and arms back to her truck where she had left her cell phone. Fueled by pure adrenaline, Ballengee rolled onto her stomach and started to crawl. For five hours she inched her way ahead. By late afternoon she had drained her water bottle, but soon afterwards she spotted a two-inch-deep ice-covered puddle. She broke through the ice and scooped out the water with her water bottle lid. She crawled a bit further but then stopped, knowing it would be dangerous to

keep going in the dark. Ballengee had covered only about 700 feet, and it was some six miles to her truck. With her body beginning to swell from internal bleeding,

*Danelle Ballangee was thankful that she had brought Taz along on her training run.*

Ballengee rolled onto her back and prepared to spend the night. She knew the worst thing she could do was to lie still, so she did little exercises to keep warm, wiggling her fingers inside her clothes, tapping her feet, and doing mini sit-ups by lifting her head a few inches. The pain was intense and constant.

6     All through the night, Ballengee did these exercises, talked to Taz, and counted the shooting stars. On Thursday morning, she ate one of her energy gels and again tried to crawl, but by this time she was too weak to make real progress. Instead, she clawed her way back to the little water hole and prepared to spend a second night in the 20-degree wilderness. She knew that if help didn't arrive soon, she would die. Somehow she survived that night, but by Friday morning her hands were numb from the cold, and she was too weak even to do her mini sit-ups. She ate the second energy gel, but she knew that she would never make it through a third night. It was then that she saw Taz run off. Despite her pain

she felt a rush of hope. Could it be that he was going for help?

7     Meanwhile, the rescue party was about to head out. Just before they left, they were surprised to see a dog running toward them from far off. The dog reached the searchers, turned, and ran back in the direction from which he had come. Again he ran to the searchers and then ran back. John Marshall, the head of the rescue party, believed that the dog was Ballengee's. After the dog approached and ran back a third time, Marshall gave the order to follow him.

8     Searcher Bego Gerhart was following the dog on foot, and he was falling behind. But then, all of a sudden Gerhart discerned three sets of prints in the dirt, all headed in the same direction. As a trained desert tracker, Gerhart could tell that one was a set of fresh dog tracks and one was a set of dog tracks about two days old. Next to the older track was a set of shoe prints. Gerhart rushed back to get his all-terrain vehicle and follow the tracks. After some time on the trail, he saw a woman on the ground in

the distance. It was Danelle Ballengee, and she was still alive! Taz was resting his head on Ballengee's chest. Tears rolled down Ballengee's cheeks as she greeted Gerhart with these simple words, "I'm glad to see you." She had survived 52 freezing hours in the mountain wilderness, and now she and the dog that had saved her life would soon be going home. ✳

*If you have been timed while reading this article, enter your reading time below. Then turn to the Words-per-Minute Table on page 101 and look up your reading speed (words per minute). Enter your reading speed on the graph on page 102.*

**Reading Time: Lesson 9**

_____ : _____

*Minutes*          *Seconds*

# A Finding the Main Idea

One statement below expresses the main idea of the article. One statement is too general, or too broad. The other statement explains only part of the article; it is too narrow. Label the statements using the following key:

**M—Main Idea**    **B—Too Broad**    **N—Too Narrow**

_____ 1. A runner, badly injured on a mountain trail, managed to stay alive for two days and was finally rescued.

_____ 2. When Danelle Ballengee fell on a mountain trail, she shattered her pelvis in four places and cracked it in others.

_____ 3. Even the most capable athlete can find herself in a life-or-death situation when alone in the wilderness.

_____ Score 15 points for a correct M answer.

_____ Score 5 points for each correct B or N answer.

_____ **Total Score**: Finding the Main Idea

# B Recalling Facts

How well do you remember the facts in the article? Put an X in the box next to the answer that correctly completes each statement about the article.

1. Ballengee excelled at the sport of
☐ a. mountain climbing.
☐ b. adventure racing.
☐ c. high jumping.

2. Ballengee had established a women's record by
☐ a. hiking up and down all of Colorado's 54 peaks.
☐ b. climbing the three highest peaks in the world.
☐ c. bicycling across the United States in the fastest time.

3. Ballengee could not use her cell phone because
☐ a. it had been shattered in the fall.
☐ b. she had left it in her truck.
☐ c. she had lost it on the trail.

4. To stay warm at night, Ballengee
☐ a. built a small fire.
☐ b. did exercises.
☐ c. drank hot coffee from an insulated bottle.

5. Searchers found Ballengee by following
☐ a. specially trained bloodhounds, which caught her scent.
☐ b. the sound of her voice.
☐ c. her dog, who ran back to her.

Score 5 points for each correct answer.

_____ **Total Score**: Recalling Facts

## C Making Inferences

When you combine your own experiences and information from a text to draw a conclusion that is not directly stated in that text, you are making an inference. Below are five statements that may or may not be inferences based on information in the article. Label the statements using the following key:

**C—Correct Inference**          **F—Faulty Inference**

_____ 1. If Ballengee's neighbor had not been so attentive, Ballengee probably would have died in the wilderness.

_____ 2. Ballengee's reputation as an adventurer helped rescuers figure out where she might be.

_____ 3. The fact that Ballengee's accident occurred in the winter improved her chances of surviving.

_____ 4. Ballengee will never jog again without bringing along her dog.

_____ 5. Ballengee had an amazing ability to think clearly in spite of terrible pain.

> Score 5 points for each correct answer.
>
> _____ **Total Score**: Making Inferences

## D Using Words Precisely

Each numbered sentence below contains an underlined word or phrase from the article. Following the sentence are three definitions. One definition is closest to the meaning of the underlined word. One definition is opposite or nearly opposite. Label those two definitions using the following key. Do not label the remaining definition.

**C—Closest**          **O—Opposite or Nearly Opposite**

1. Ballengee has had several <u>dramatic</u> triumphs.

   _____ a. remarkable and exciting

   _____ b. difficult to understand

   _____ c. commonplace and boring

2. There she planned to cover part of a trail called Amasa Back, a popular route during warmer months, and then to split off onto some <u>obscure</u>, unmapped trails known only to locals.

   _____ a. far from major cities

   _____ b. famous

   _____ c. unknown to most people

3. Ballengee plunged 60 feet nearly straight down, crashing into three <u>successive</u> rock faces before hitting the bottom of the canyon.

   _____ a. happening all at the same time

   _____ b. sharp and jagged

   _____ c. following one after the other

4. The horrific fall shattered her pelvis in four places and cracked it in others, leaving the bottom half of her body nearly <u>immobile</u>.

   _____ a. moving constantly

   _____ b. unable to move

   _____ c. separated

5. All of a sudden Gerhart <u>discerned</u> three sets of prints in the dirt, all headed in the same direction.

_____ a.   recognized through study

_____ b.   overlooked

_____ c.   covered up

_____ Score 3 points for each correct C answer.

_____ Score 2 points for each correct O answer.

_____ **Total Score**: Using Words Precisely

Enter the four total scores in the spaces below, and add them together to find your Reading Comprehension Score. Then record your score on the graph on page 103.

| Score | Question Type | Lesson 9 |
|---|---|---|
| _____ | Finding the Main Idea | |
| _____ | Recalling Facts | |
| _____ | Making Inferences | |
| _____ | Using Words Precisely | |
| _____ | **Reading Comprehension Score** | |

## Author's Approach

Put an X in the box next to the correct answer.

1. The author uses the first sentence of the article to
   - ☐ a.   hint that something bad might have happened to Ballengee.
   - ☐ b.   describe Ballengee's home.
   - ☐ c.   show that Ballengee's neighbor was nosy.

2. The author probably wrote this article in order to
   - ☐ a.   persuade the reader not to hike alone in the wilderness.
   - ☐ b.   tell an exciting story of survival.
   - ☐ c.   show how wonderful it is to own a good dog.

3. The author tells this story mainly by
   - ☐ a.   retelling personal experiences.
   - ☐ b.   comparing different topics.
   - ☐ c.   describing events in the order they happened.

4. What does the author imply by saying "Just before they left, they were surprised to see a dog running toward them from far off"?
   - ☐ a.   They were afraid that the dog was going to attack them.
   - ☐ b.   They thought that the dog was frightened by something in that direction.
   - ☐ c.   They thought it was unusual to see a friendly dog without an owner in that remote area.

_____ Number of correct answers

Record your personal assessment of your work on the Critical Thinking Chart on page 104.

**CRITICAL THINKING**

# Summarizing and Paraphrasing

Put an X in the box next to the correct answer.

1. Choose the best one-sentence paraphrase for the following sentence from the article: "By late afternoon she had drained her water bottle, but soon afterwards she spotted a two-inch-deep ice-covered puddle."

☐ a. Even though she had found an ice-covered puddle, she continued to drink from her water bottle until it was empty.

☐ b. All day she drank from her water bottle, not knowing that there was an ice-covered puddle nearby.

☐ c. She had drunk all her water by late in the afternoon, but eventually found a shallow, ice-covered puddle.

2. Read the statement about the article below. Then read the paraphrase of that statement. Choose the reason that best tells why the paraphrase does not say the same thing as the statement.

Statement: Although Ballengee had worked for five hours to get back to her truck, she had traveled only 700 feet, and the truck was six miles away.

Paraphrase: After crawling for five hours, Ballengee was able to get only 700 feet closer to her truck, which was six miles away, and so she gave up for the night.

☐ a. Paraphrase says too much.

☐ b. Paraphrase doesn't say enough.

☐ c. Paraphrase doesn't agree with the statement.

_____ Number of correct answers

Record your personal assessment of your work on the Critical Thinking Chart on page 104.

# Critical Thinking

Follow the directions provided for questions 1 and 5. Put an X next to the correct answer for the other questions.

1. For each statement below, write O if it expresses an opinion or write F if it expresses a fact.

_____ a. It is amazing that Danelle Ballengee kept a level head and did not panic after her accident.

_____ b. Mixed breeds, such as Taz, are the smartest dogs.

_____ c. Ballengee won the Pikes Peak Marathon four times.

2. From the article, you can predict that if Ballengee goes running in the mountains alone again, she will

☐ a. take enough food and water to last about three days.

☐ b. notify the local police.

☐ c. bring along some kind of instrument that she can use to signal or call for help if needed.

3. What was the effect of Ballengee's injuries?

☐ a. She couldn't crawl or roll over.

☐ b. She couldn't stand up or walk.

☐ c. She couldn't think clearly.

4. Judging by events in the article, you can conclude that

☐ a. Taz was a smart and faithful dog whom Ballengee treated well.

☐ b. Adventure racing should be outlawed in Utah.

☐ c. To stay safe in the wilderness, every adventurer should travel with a dog.

5. Which paragraphs provide evidence that supports your answer to question 3?

_____

_____

```
_____  Number of correct answers

Record your personal assessment of your work on the Critical
Thinking Chart on page 104.
```

## Personal Response

Begin the first 5–8 sentences of your own article about an accident and a rescue. It may tell of a real experience or one that is imagined.

_____

_____

_____

_____

_____

_____

_____

_____

## Self-Assessment

I really can't understand how

_____

_____

_____

_____

_____

_____

_____

_____

_____

_____

_____

_____

_____

_____

CRITICAL THINKING

# Trapped

*Coyotes usually hunt in groups of two or three. They will eat almost anything, especially if the prey is wounded and can't run.*

Ken Hildebrand, a volunteer emergency medical technician and licensed trapper, knew how to pack for any emergency. So on January 8, 2008, when he headed out to inspect his beaver traps, the 55-year-old Canadian was prepared. Hildebrand was headed for the Livingstone Gap area of the Rocky Mountains, about 80 miles southwest of Calgary, Alberta. He packed his four-wheeled all-terrain vehicle (ATV) carefully because he planned to camp out for several nights. He stocked it with plenty of food and water, a first-aid kit, an axe, and a sleeping bag good enough for temperatures as low as 40 degrees below zero. In fact, Hildebrand packed enough supplies to survive in the winter wilderness for many days. Sometimes, however, even the best-laid plans are not enough.

2    Out in the Gap, Hildebrand collected a couple of dead beavers from his traps and then remounted his ATV. The terrain was very rugged and the wind was blowing hard. As Hildebrand bounced along, a piece of dirt or grass flew into his eye. For just a moment he took one hand off the handlebar to wipe his eye. In that brief moment, he struck a rock, and the heavily loaded ATV flipped over. Hildebrand was sent tumbling down the hillside, with the ATV bouncing wildly down behind him. When he landed at the bottom of the hill, the ATV rolled right on top of him, pinning his legs and leaving him face-down on the frozen ground. Hildebrand felt excruciating pain in his right leg, which was bearing much of the vehicle's weight. His left leg, which was badly shriveled from childhood polio, was pinned under his right leg.

3    Hildebrand tried to push the ATV off, but it wouldn't budge. That's when he knew that if he was going to make it out of there alive he would have to go into "survival mode." Most of the supplies were still tied securely to the ATV, but they were out of reach. The only useful tool he thought he might be able to grab was his axe, which had fallen on the ground just inches beyond his outstretched hand. Using a string that he had tied around his neck, he was able to lasso the axe and pull it toward him.

Hildebrand then tried to swing the axe up toward the cords holding his supplies, but his awkward hacks at the cords only managed to cut loose the dead beavers. Next he tried to use the axe handle as a lever to lift the ATV off his body. Using all his might, he did manage to lift the vehicle a couple of inches, but then the axe handle snapped off in his hands. That left him with no chance of wriggling out from under the vehicle. He also had little hope that a search party would find him soon, since his family and friends were not expecting him home for days.

4    As night fell, Hildebrand could see lights in a farmhouse only about a half mile away.

*Ken Hildebrand survived 96 hours trapped under his ATV in the Canadian Rocky Mountains.*

He blew his emergency whistle, which started the farmer's dogs barking, but the farmer apparently never heard the whistle in the high winds. Meanwhile Hildebrand understood that no matter what else happened he could not fall asleep. If he did, he knew that, with temperatures dipping to 11 degrees below zero, he would soon succumb to hypothermia. Reflecting back on his work as a rescue worker, Hildebrand later said, "During my 15 years on rescue, I probably saw three or four people that were in my situation, and none of them survived."

5    Hildebrand knew he needed to stay warm and do what he could to keep his strength up. He had a knife with him and thought about using it to skin one of the beavers. The animal's flesh would provide him some nourishment, and its fur could help insulate parts of his body from the cold. But Hildebrand also knew that the smell of a bloody beaver carcass would attract coyotes or maybe even a cougar. Unable to move, and with his axe handle broken, he would have no way to defend himself if wild animals attacked. "Had I been attacked by a cougar, my chances would have been zero," he later said.

6    After weighing his chances, Hildebrand decided it was worth the risk. He partly skinned one of the beavers and ate a few bites of the meat. Unfortunately, this only made him sick to his stomach, and he vomited, leaving him in even weaker condition. Hildebrand managed to place the remainder of the carcass below his waist with the fur side up, and this provided him with a little warmth. He also was able to gather a tiny bit of water by laying strips of plastic surveyor's tape on the ground to collect frost. Hildebrand first arranged the bright orange plastic strips in an X in case a passing aircraft would see it from above. In the mornings, he ran the strips through his teeth, licking off the frost that had collected during the night. Then he set the tape back out again at arm's length. Although Hildebrand survived the first night and the next day, he wasn't sure how long he could last without food and with very little water.

7    On the second night, the scent of the beaver meat attracted a pack of coyotes. He was able to drive the animals away by shouting at them, blowing the whistle, and banging the axe handle on the side of the ATV. Just before daybreak, the coyotes returned, and Hildebrand again held them off. On the third night, the coyotes crept up again, this time from behind him. Hildebrand listened to their yipping noises and their feet scraping the hard ground, and he tried to imagine what would happen next. "They were definitely excited, and they were getting each other excited," Hildebrand said. Then some of the coyotes began fighting over a beaver carcass. Other coyotes began lunging and snapping at Hildebrand. Once more he held them off by making noises and swinging the axe handle. The dogs at the farmhouse took up barking again, and after some time, the pack of coyotes ran off.

8    By the morning of the fourth day, Hildebrand's strength was gone and his body began to shut down. Now, for the first time in four days, he took off his glasses, closed his eyes, and fell asleep.

9    That should have been the end of the story for Ken Hildebrand, except for an odd piece of luck. Roy Davidson was out walking with his dog that morning, and he had decided to hike through Livingstone Gap, an area where he had never gone before. As he walked to the bottom of a ravine, Davidson spotted Hildebrand lying under his ATV. Davidson rushed over and flipped the vehicle off Hildebrand, who was just barely alive.

10    Ken Hildebrand had survived 96 terrifying hours in the freezing cold and was dehydrated, frostbitten, half-frozen, and starving. The doctors had to cut off his right leg, which had been crushed by the weight of the ATV. "I think the reason that Ken survived is he's tough." Davidson said. "He's one tough dude." ✳

---

*If you have been timed while reading this article, enter your reading time below. Then turn to the Words-per-Minute Table on page 101 and look up your reading speed (words per minute). Enter your reading speed on the graph on page 102.*

**Reading Time: Lesson 10**

_____ : _____
*Minutes*         *Seconds*

## A Finding the Main Idea

One statement below expresses the main idea of the article. One statement is too general, or too broad. The other statement explains only part of the article; it is too narrow. Label the statements using the following key:

**M—Main Idea**    **B—Too Broad**    **N—Too Narrow**

_____ 1.  Ken Hildebrand, a licensed beaver trapper in Canada, ran into trouble when he crashed his ATV.

_____ 2.  Ken Hildebrand skinned a beaver for its fur and meat when he became trapped in the Canadian Rockies.

_____ 3.  Ken Hildebrand was trapped under his ATV but managed to survive 96 hours in freezing cold weather.

_____ Score 15 points for a correct M answer.

_____ Score 5 points for each correct B or N answer.

_____ **Total Score**: Finding the Main Idea

## B Recalling Facts

How well do you remember the facts in the article? Put an X in the box next to the answer that correctly completes each statement about the article.

1.  Hildebrand's ATV flipped when
    ☐ a.  a strong wind blew it over.
    ☐ b.  Hildebrand struck a rock.
    ☐ c.  Hildebrand drove it down a hillside.

2.  Hildebrand ate only a few bites of beaver meat because
    ☐ a.  the raw meat made him sick.
    ☐ b.  the coyotes took it from him.
    ☐ c.  he could not cut the meat well with an axe.

3.  Hildebrand was able to get some water from
    ☐ a.  melting snow.
    ☐ b.  a water bottle he lassoed from the ATV.
    ☐ c.  strips of surveyor's tape that had collected frost.

4.  The scent of beaver meat attracted
    ☐ a.  a pack of coyotes.
    ☐ b.  a cougar.
    ☐ c.  dogs from a nearby farmhouse.

5.  Roy Davidson found Hildebrand because he
    ☐ a.  had been looking for Hildebrand.
    ☐ b.  was out walking his dog in the area.
    ☐ c.  heard Hildebrand's whistle and the banging noises.

Score 5 points for each correct answer.

_____ **Total Score**: Recalling Facts

## C Making Inferences

When you combine your own experiences and information from a text to draw a conclusion that is not directly stated in that text, you are making an inference. Below are five statements that may or may not be inferences based on information in the article. Label the statements using the following key:

C—Correct Inference          F—Faulty Inference

_____  1.  If Hildebrand had a cell phone, he was not able to reach it.

_____  2.  Coyotes have an excellent sense of smell.

_____  3.  ATVs are very difficult to drive.

_____  4.  The farmer who owned the dogs probably heard Hildebrand's whistle but chose not to come out.

_____  5.  Hildebrand was taking an extreme risk by going out alone with a weak leg.

---

Score 5 points for each correct answer.

_____ **Total Score**: Making Inferences

---

## D Using Words Precisely

Each numbered sentence below contains an underlined word or phrase from the article. Following the sentence are three definitions. One definition is closest to the meaning of the underlined word. One definition is opposite or nearly opposite. Label those two definitions using the following key. Do not label the remaining definition.

C—Closest          O—Opposite or Nearly Opposite

1.  Hildebrand felt excruciating pain in his right leg.

    _____  a.  delightful, pleasing

    _____  b.  unexpected, surprising

    _____  c.  intense or extreme

2.  Hildebrand knew that if he fell asleep, he would soon succumb to hypothermia.

    _____  a.  dream about

    _____  b.  give in

    _____  c.  resist

3.  The animal's fur could help insulate parts of his body from the cold.

    _____  a.  pass over

    _____  b.  allow or let in

    _____  c.  protect, cover up

4.  As he walked to the bottom of a ravine, Davidson spotted Hildebrand lying under his ATV.

    _____  a.  mountain ridge

    _____  b.  deep, narrow valley

    _____  c.  rocky trail

5. Hildebrand was <u>dehydrated</u>, frostbitten, half-frozen, and starving.

_____ a. suffering from lack of water

_____ b. badly cut

_____ c. given enough water

---

_____ Score 3 points for each correct C answer.

_____ Score 2 points for each correct O answer.

_____ **Total Score**: Using Words Precisely

---

Enter the four total scores in the spaces below, and add them together to find your Reading Comprehension Score. Then record your score on the graph on page 103.

| Score | Question Type | Lesson 10 |
|---|---|---|
| _____ | Finding the Main Idea | |
| _____ | Recalling Facts | |
| _____ | Making Inferences | |
| _____ | Using Words Precisely | |
| _____ | **Reading Comprehension Score** | |

## Author's Approach

Put an X in the box next to the correct answer.

1. What is the author's purpose in writing this article?
☐ a. to criticize those who trap wild animals
☐ b. to inspire the reader by telling a story about a man who survived despite great odds.
☐ c. to explain that trouble can happen even to those who are well prepared.

2. What does the author imply by saying "Now, for the first time in four days, Hildebrand took off his glasses, closed his eyes, and fell asleep"?
☐ a. He had given up hope that he could escape or be rescued.
☐ b. His eye hurt from whatever had flown into it.
☐ c. Since the beaver furs kept him warm, he could sleep.

3. Judging by statements from the article "Trapped," you can conclude that the author wants the reader to think that Hildebrand
☐ a. was brave and resourceful.
☐ b. caused his own problems.
☐ c. did not plan his trip well.

4. Which of the following statements from the article best describes Ken Hildebrand?
☐ a. "That's when he knew that if he was going to make it out of there alive he would have to go into 'survival mode.'"
☐ b. "He's one tough dude."
☐ c. "Meanwhile Hildebrand knew that no matter what else happened, he could not fall asleep."

_____ Number of correct answers

Record your personal assessment of your work on the Critical Thinking Chart on page 104.

**CRITICAL THINKING**

# Summarizing and Paraphrasing

Put an X in the box next to the correct answer for questions 1 and 2. Follow the directions provided for question 3.

1. Read the statement from the article below. Then read the paraphrase of that statement. Choose the reason that best tells why the paraphrase does not say the same thing as the statement.

   Statement: Hildebrand packed enough supplies to survive in the wilderness for many days.

   Paraphrase: Because Hildebrand spent a lot of time in the wilderness, he knew how to pack for his trip.

   ☐ a. Paraphrase says too much.

   ☐ b. Paraphrase doesn't say enough.

   ☐ c. Paraphrase doesn't agree with the statement.

2. Choose the sentence that correctly restates the following sentence from the article: "Sometimes, however, even the best-laid plans are not enough."

   ☐ a. From time to time, people do not make arrangements well enough in advance.

   ☐ b. Occasionally, people do not think ahead.

   ☐ c. There are times when, despite a great deal of planning for an event, something unexpected occurs.

3. Reread paragraph 2 in the article. Below, write a summary of the paragraph in no more than 25 words.

   _____

   _____

   _____

   _____

   _____

   _____ Number of correct answers

   Record your personal assessment of your work on the Critical Thinking Chart on page 104.

# Critical Thinking

Put an X in the box next to the correct answer for questions 1 and 4. Follow the directions provided for the other questions.

1. Which of the following statements from the article is an opinion rather than a fact?

   ☐ a. "The doctors had to cut off his right leg, which had been crushed by the weight of the ATV."

   ☐ b. "I think the reason that Ken survived is he's tough."

   ☐ c. "The terrain was very rugged and the wind was blowing hard."

2. Choose from the letters below to correctly complete the following statement. Write the letters on the lines.

   According to the article, _____ caused the ATV to _____, and the effect was _____.

   a. flip over

   b. striking a rock

   c. the ATV tumbled to the bottom of a hill

CRITICAL THINKING

3. Of the following theme categories, which would this story fit into?

   a. man against nature

   b. might makes right

   c. nothing in life is free

4. Judging by events in the article, you can conclude that

   ☐ a. the people in the nearby farmhouse would have finally rescued Hildebrand.

   ☐ b. trapping beavers is a very dangerous activity.

   ☐ c. Hildebrand's survival was due to a combination of his determination and sheer luck.

5. In which paragraph did you find your information or details to answer question 2?

   _____

   _____ Number of correct answers

   Record your personal assessment of your work on the Critical Thinking Chart on page 104.

## Personal Response

If I were the author, I would add

_____

_____

_____

_____

## Self-Assessment

From reading this article, I have learned

_____

_____

_____

_____

_____

_____

_____

_____

# Compare and Contrast

Think about the articles you have read in Unit Two. Choose three articles that would be the most frightening. Write the titles of the articles in the first column of the chart below. Use information you learned from the articles to fill in the empty boxes in the chart.

| Title | Could this situation have been avoided? Why or why not? | What advice would you have given that would have relieved or solved the problem? | What was the key action or decision that made survival possible? |
|---|---|---|---|
| | | | |
| | | | |
| | | | |

How did the survivor's character play a major role in his or her survival? _____

_____

_____

_____.

# Words-per-Minute Table

## Unit Two

**Directions** If you were timed while reading an article, refer to the Reading Time you recorded in the box at the end of the article. Use this words-per-minute table to determine your reading speed for that article. Then plot your reading speed on the graph on page 102.

| Lesson | 6 | 7 | 8 | 9 | 10 | |
|---|---|---|---|---|---|---|
| No. of Words | 1163 | 1155 | 1153 | 1124 | 1197 | |
| 1:30 | 775 | 770 | 769 | 749 | 798 | 90 |
| 1:40 | 698 | 693 | 692 | 674 | 718 | 100 |
| 1:50 | 634 | 630 | 629 | 613 | 653 | 110 |
| 2:00 | 582 | 578 | 577 | 562 | 599 | 120 |
| 2:10 | 537 | 533 | 532 | 519 | 552 | 130 |
| 2:20 | 498 | 495 | 494 | 482 | 513 | 140 |
| 2:30 | 465 | 462 | 461 | 450 | 479 | 150 |
| 2:40 | 436 | 433 | 432 | 422 | 449 | 160 |
| 2:50 | 410 | 408 | 407 | 397 | 422 | 170 |
| 3:00 | 388 | 385 | 384 | 375 | 399 | 180 |
| 3:10 | 367 | 365 | 364 | 355 | 378 | 190 |
| 3:20 | 349 | 347 | 346 | 337 | 359 | 200 |
| 3:30 | 332 | 330 | 329 | 321 | 342 | 210 |
| 3:40 | 317 | 315 | 314 | 307 | 326 | 220 |
| 3:50 | 303 | 301 | 301 | 293 | 312 | 230 |
| 4:00 | 291 | 289 | 288 | 281 | 299 | 240 |
| 4:10 | 279 | 277 | 277 | 270 | 287 | 250 |
| 4:20 | 268 | 267 | 266 | 259 | 276 | 260 |
| 4:30 | 258 | 257 | 256 | 250 | 266 | 270 |
| 4:40 | 249 | 248 | 247 | 241 | 257 | 280 |
| 4:50 | 241 | 239 | 239 | 233 | 248 | 290 |
| 5:00 | 233 | 231 | 231 | 225 | 239 | 300 |
| 5:10 | 225 | 224 | 223 | 218 | 232 | 310 |
| 5:20 | 218 | 217 | 216 | 211 | 224 | 320 |
| 5:30 | 211 | 210 | 210 | 204 | 218 | 330 |
| 5:40 | 205 | 204 | 203 | 198 | 211 | 340 |
| 5:50 | 199 | 198 | 198 | 193 | 205 | 350 |
| 6:00 | 194 | 193 | 192 | 187 | 200 | 360 |
| 6:10 | 189 | 187 | 187 | 182 | 194 | 370 |
| 6:20 | 184 | 182 | 182 | 177 | 189 | 380 |
| 6:30 | 179 | 178 | 177 | 173 | 184 | 390 |
| 6:40 | 174 | 173 | 173 | 169 | 180 | 400 |
| 6:50 | 170 | 169 | 169 | 164 | 175 | 410 |
| 7:00 | 166 | 165 | 165 | 161 | 171 | 420 |
| 7:10 | 162 | 161 | 161 | 157 | 167 | 430 |
| 7:20 | 159 | 158 | 157 | 153 | 163 | 440 |
| 7:30 | 155 | 154 | 154 | 150 | 160 | 450 |
| 7:40 | 152 | 151 | 150 | 147 | 156 | 460 |
| 7:50 | 148 | 147 | 147 | 143 | 153 | 470 |
| 8:00 | 145 | 144 | 144 | 141 | 150 | 480 |

Minutes and Seconds

Seconds

# Plotting Your Progress: Reading Speed

## Unit Two

**Directions** If you were timed while reading an article, write your words-per-minute rate for that article in the box under the number of the lesson. Then plot your reading speed on the graph by putting a small X on the line directly above the number of the lesson, across from the number of words per minute you read. As you mark your speed for each lesson, graph your progress by drawing a line to connect the Xs.

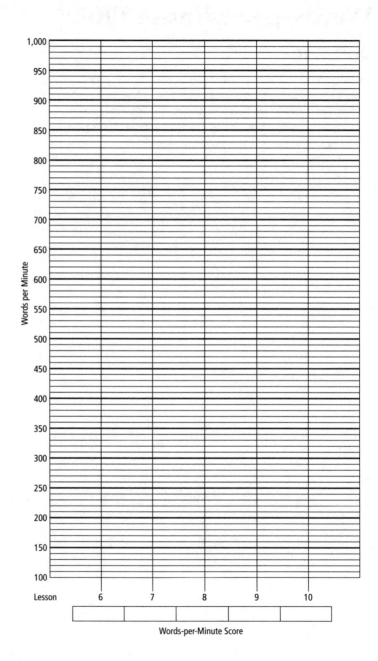

Words-per-Minute Score

# Plotting Your Progress: Reading Comprehension

## Unit Two

**Directions** Write your Reading Comprehension score for each lesson in the box under the number of the lesson. Then plot your score on the graph by putting a small X on the line directly above the number of the lesson and across from the score you earned. As you mark your score for each lesson, graph your progress by drawing a line to connect the Xs.

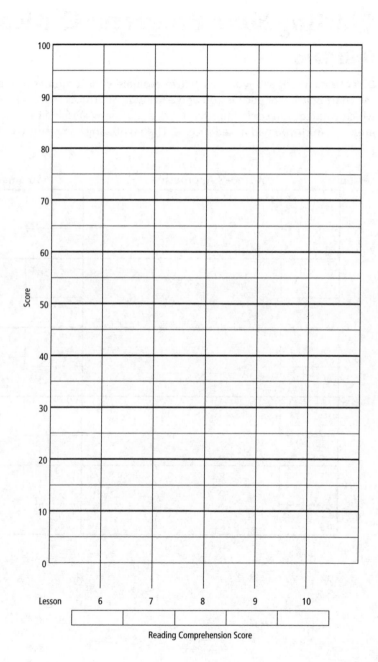

Lesson    6    7    8    9    10

Reading Comprehension Score

# Plotting Your Progress: Critical Thinking

## Unit Two

**Directions** Work with your teacher to evaluate your responses to the Critical Thinking questions for each lesson. Then fill in the appropriate spaces in the chart below. For each lesson and each type of Critical Thinking question, do the following: Mark a minus sign (–) in the box to indicate areas in which you feel you could improve. Mark a plus sign (+) to indicate areas in which you feel you did well. Mark a minus-slash-plus sign (–/+) to indicate areas in which you had mixed success. Then write any comments you have about your performance, including ideas for improvement.

| Lesson | Author's Approach | Summarizing and Paraphrasing | Critical Thinking |
|--------|-------------------|------------------------------|-------------------|
| 6 | | | |
| 7 | | | |
| 8 | | | |
| 9 | | | |
| 10 | | | |

# Unit Three

# Taken Hostage

*An airplane flies over a coca field in Colombia where three Americans were taken hostage.*

On February 13, 2003, five men took off in a single-engine plane to go on a routine inspection flight over the jungles of Colombia, South America. Three of the men, Americans Marc Gonsalves, Keith Stansell, and Tom Howes, had been hired by a global security company called Northrup Grumman, which had a contract with the U.S. government to provide airborne surveillance of Colombian drug dealers. What they and American pilot Tom Janis and a Colombian army intelligence officer, Sgt. Luis Alcides Cruz, were looking for were coca fields that were maintained and guarded by drug traffickers. The organizations that control these fields harvest the crops to make cocaine, which is then trafficked illegally into the United States. On this particular day, the men weren't looking for trouble, nor did they expect any. However, they did find it, and for the next several years they were forced to pay the price.

2    While the men scouted a coca field, the plane's engine failed, and Janis was forced to crash-land very near where traffickers were gathered. All of the men survived the sudden landing, but Gonsalves, Stansell, and Howes were badly injured in the crash. The plane was immediately surrounded by members of the notorious Revolutionary

Armed Forces of Colombia (FARC). The FARC is the military wing of a terrorist group that has been at war with the Colombian government since 1964. To finance its military operations, the FARC often resorted to drug trafficking and kidnapping for ransom. If the stranded men had any doubt about the danger they were in, it was dispelled when the FARC rebels walked up to Tom Janis and Sgt. Alcides Cruz and immediately executed them. They wanted the other three men alive; the Americans would be valuable bargaining chips in future negotiations with the Colombian government.

3    For Gonsalves, Stansell, and Howes, that was the beginning of 1,967 days as hostages in the South American rain forest. The rebels forced the Americans to set off on a brutally long march to get as far away as possible from the crash site. The group would arrive at one place, and then pick up and move to another, and then another. For the next five and a half years, the FARC rebels constantly moved the three men from place to place in order to keep one step ahead of the Colombian military. Often the men were linked to one another by a heavy chain around their necks. During their long captivity, Gonsalves, Stansell, and Howes, periodically suffered from starvation, illness, and isolation from one another.

4    The FARC rebels had other hostages too, and at times the Americans were joined by more than a dozen others. One of the hostages was Ingrid Betancourt, who was kidnapped while she campaigned for the Colombian presidency. Many others were captured Colombian soldiers, and one hostage was a pregnant woman who gave birth during her captivity.

5    Day after day, the hostages struggled to survive. When they were not marching, Gonsalves, Stansell, and Howes sometimes were allowed to play chess or exercise by lifting weights. They carved the chess pieces out of wood and cut hand grips into logs to use for barbells. The men also talked about what they would do when they returned to their families in the United States. Their dream-filled conversations often returned to a favorite topic, a motorcycle trip they would take together across the United States. They even allowed themselves to imagine details of the trip, such as the types of restaurants they would stop at along the way. Just the thought of what they called their "freedom ride" helped them to cope with the cruel realities of their jungle captivity.

6    Meanwhile, the Colombian military was actively pursuing the FARC rebels. Sometimes the Americans saw government helicopters overhead, and when that happened the rebels forced the hostages to

*Stansell, Gonsalves, and Howes were photographed by FARC rebels while being held for more than five years.*

march to some other hidden prison camp. Each helicopter sighting produced a mixture of hope and fear in the captives. Of course they wanted to be rescued, but they also believed that the rebels would kill them if the Colombian army moved in. As Gonsalves later said about one of his rebel guards, "It was his mission to prevent me from going home." This guard, Alexander Farfan, often boasted to the hostages that he would never be taken alive. "I will fight to the death!" he kept repeating.

7     Occasionally the rebels would invite outsiders to visit the prison camps. Their purpose was to have them film "proof-of-life" videos that could be used in ransom negotiations. When the Americans refused to say they were being treated well by their captors or recite what they were told to say in front of the camera, the rebels beat them.

8     By 2008 constant pressure by the Colombian military had greatly reduced the power and influence of the FARC. Death and desertion had reduced the FARC's size from roughly 20,000 members a decade earlier to about 10,000. In addition, two top leaders had been killed, which further weakened the movement. In the absence of these leaders, it became easier for secret agents of the Colombian military to carry out a bold plan. First, they would penetrate the inner circles of the FARC leadership to gain information then attack the rebels when they were not expecting it.

9     The secret agents spent months gaining the trust of the men who were holding Gonsalves, Stansell, and Howes. Finally, they saw an opportunity, and they made their move. With the FARC's approval, the agents made arrangements for an "international mission" to visit the hostages. The rebels believed that a proof-of-life video made by an international film crew would help their cause. They agreed to round up the hostages and march them to the assigned meeting place, which was more than 90 miles away. When they arrived at the place, the hostages were separated into three groups. A large unmarked helicopter carrying Colombian security forces disguised as FARC supporters swooped down to meet them. Thinking that the helicopter would take them to meet the international film crew, Farfan and another rebel climbed aboard, pulling the three Americans and Betancourt on with them. Once in the air, the agents pounced on the two guards. One struggled mightily until the soldiers knocked him unconscious. But Farfan, who had boasted he would never be taken alive, did nothing, and the soldiers placed him in handcuffs.

The slick rescue operation, known as Checkmate, went off so perfectly that none of the hostages was injured. The Colombian President Álvaro Uribe called the mission "an unbelievable military achievement."

10     As for Gonsalves, Stansell, and Howes, their achievement was that they managed to survive more than five years of jungle captivity. Throughout years of physical pain and emotional and mental stress, the three men took care of each other, stood up to their captors, and held on to hope. Their strong will and courage turned out to be enough to see them home. ✳

*If you have been timed while reading this article, enter your reading time below. Then turn to the Words-per-Minute Table on page 147 and look up your reading speed (words per minute). Enter your reading speed on the graph on page 148.*

**Reading Time: Lesson 11**

_____ : _____

*Minutes*          *Seconds*

# A | Finding the Main Idea

One statement below expresses the main idea of the article. One statement is too general, or too broad. The other statement explains only part of the article; it is too narrow. Label the statements using the following key:

**M—Main Idea**     **B—Too Broad**     **N—Too Narrow**

_____  1.  Three American hostages in Colombia survived for years despite cruel treatment from their terrorist captors.

_____  2.  To survive in the rain forest of South America, three American hostages often entertained themselves by planning a motorcycle trip across the United States.

_____  3.  Rebel terrorists are often harsh and cruel in their treatment of hostages.

_____  Score 15 points for a correct M answer.

_____  Score 5 points for each correct B or N answer.

_____  **Total Score:** Finding the Main Idea

# B | Recalling Facts

How well do you remember the facts in the article? Put an X in the box next to the answer that correctly completes each statement about the article.

1.  The three Americans were taken hostage in
☐  a.  2001.
☐  b.  2003.
☐  c.  2008.

2.  The Americans were prisoners for
☐  a.  five and a half years.
☐  b.  two years.
☐  c.  967 days.

3.  Another hostage was Ingrid Betancourt, who
☐  a.  was a Columbian pop singer.
☐  b.  was pregnant and gave birth.
☐  c.  had been running for president of Colombia.

4.  Alexander Farfan was
☐  a.  the pilot of the surveillance plane.
☐  b.  a boastful guard.
☐  c.  commander of the FARC unit.

5.  Secret agents pretended they wanted to take the hostages to
☐  a.  a visit with an international film crew.
☐  b.  the capital city to meet the Colombian president.
☐  c.  a local television station to be interviewed.

Score 5 points for each correct answer.

_____  **Total Score:** Recalling Facts

## C Making Inferences

When you combine your own experiences and information from a text to draw a conclusion that is not directly stated in that text, you are making an inference. Below are five statements that may or may not be inferences based on information in the article. Label the statements using the following key:

**C—Correct Inference**          **F—Faulty Inference**

_____ 1. The FARC terrorists were probably surprised when the Americans' plane crash-landed near their camp.

_____ 2. The three Americans built a strong relationship with each other while they were held hostage.

_____ 3. The American hostages were too injured in the crash to walk very far.

_____ 4. No one in the United States was aware that the men were taken hostage.

_____ 5. The rebels kept the American hostages busy every minute of the day.

---

Score 5 points for each correct answer.

_____ **Total Score**: Making Inferences

---

## D Using Words Precisely

Each numbered sentence below contains an underlined word or phrase from the article. Following the sentence are three definitions. One definition is closest to the meaning of the underlined word. One definition is opposite or nearly opposite. Label those two definitions using the following key. Do not label the remaining definition.

**C—Closest**          **O—Opposite or Nearly Opposite**

1. The Americans had been hired by a global security company called Northrup Grumman, which had a contract with the U.S. government to provide airborne <u>surveillance</u> of Colombian drug dealers.

_____ a. destruction

_____ b. steady observation

_____ c. cover up

2. If the stranded men had any doubt about the danger they were in, it was <u>dispelled</u> when the FARC rebels walked up to Tom Janis and Sgt. Alcides Cruz and immediately executed them.

_____ a. caused to disappear

_____ b. made clearer

_____ c. communicated

3. During their long <u>captivity</u>, the men suffered from starvation, illness, and isolation from one another.

_____ a. freedom

_____ b. forced march

_____ c. imprisonment

4. Death and <u>desertion</u> had reduced the FARC's size from roughly 20,000 members a decade earlier to about 10,000.

_____ a. leaving in secret or without permission

_____ b. unknown disease

_____ c. always visible and present

5. They would <u>penetrate</u> the inner circles of the FARC leadership to gain information then attack the rebels when they were not expecting it.

_____ a. observe

_____ b. get inside

_____ c. withdraw from

_____ Score 3 points for each correct C answer.

_____ Score 2 points for each correct O answer.

_____ **Total Score:** Using Words Precisely

Enter the four total scores in the spaces below, and add them together to find your Reading Comprehension Score. Then record your score on the graph on page 149.

| Score | Question Type | Lesson 11 |
|---|---|---|
| _____ | Finding the Main Idea | |
| _____ | Recalling Facts | |
| _____ | Making Inferences | |
| _____ | Using Words Precisely | |
| _____ | **Reading Comprehension Score** | |

## Author's Approach

Put an X in the box next to the correct answer.

1. The author uses the first sentence of the article to
   ☐ a. inform the reader about the time and place of the action to follow.
   ☐ b. describe the jungles of Colombia, South America.
   ☐ c. explain why inspections were needed in Colombia.

2. What is the author's purpose in writing this article?
   ☐ a. to show how out of control the Colombia terrorist situation was during the early 2000s
   ☐ b. to inform the reader about three men who refused to give up in a terrible situation
   ☐ c. to express an opinion about whether airborne surveillance in Colombia is worthwhile

3. Choose the statement below that best describes the author's opinion in paragraph 10.
   ☐ a. The hostages felt both physical and psychological pain.
   ☐ b. The hostages survived several years in the jungle.
   ☐ c. The hostages were courageous and strong during their captivity.

4. The author tells this story mainly by
   ☐ a. retelling personal experiences.
   ☐ b. comparing different topics.
   ☐ c. describing events in the order they happened.

_____ Number of correct answers

Record your personal assessment of your work on the Critical Thinking Chart on page 150.

# Summarizing and Paraphrasing

Put an X in the box next to the correct answer.

1. Choose the best one-sentence paraphrase for the following sentence from the article: "They carved the chess pieces out of wood and cut hand grips into logs to use for barbells."

   ☐ a. To make chess pieces, they cut hand grips into logs.

   ☐ b. The chess pieces they made were cut from logs, as were their handmade barbells.

   ☐ c. They made chess pieces by carving bits of wood and fashioned barbells by cutting hand grips into logs.

2. Below are summaries of the article. Choose the summary that says all the most important things about the article but in the fewest words.

   ☐ a. Even though three Americans were taken hostage in 2003, they never gave up hope that they would one day be rescued. In a daring mission, they were rescued in 2008.

   ☐ b. Three Americans on a surveillance mission over Colombian jungles crashed near rebel terrorists. The crew of the plane were killed, but the Americans were kept alive and forced to stay with the rebels for years. Sometimes they dreamed of being rescued and celebrating their freedom with a motorcycle ride across the United States.

   ☐ c. When their plane crashed in the Colombian jungle in 2003, three Americans searching for coca fields were taken hostage by rebel terrorists. For years they were forced to move from place to place with the rebels. In 2008 they were rescued by Colombian agents.

---

_____ Number of correct answers

Record your personal assessment of your work on the Critical Thinking Chart on page 150.

---

# Critical Thinking

Follow the directions provided for questions 1, 3, and 4. Put an X next to the correct answer for the other questions.

1. For each statement below, write O if it expresses an opinion or write F if it expresses a fact.

   _____ a. The rescue operation, Checkmate, was amazingly clever and well done.

   _____ b. By 2008 the FARC had lost about half of its members.

   _____ c. Sometimes the hostages were linked to one another with a heavy chain around their necks.

2. Considering that the FARC rebels who had kidnapped the Americans were not arrested, you can predict that the Colombian military will

   ☐ a. continue fighting against the FARC rebels in the jungle.

   ☐ b. begin spying on coca fields from the ground.

   ☐ c. leave the FARC alone until the next time hostages are taken.

3. Choose from the letters below to correctly complete the following statement. Write the letter on the lines.

   On the positive side, _____, but on the negative side, _____.

   a. the three Americans were held hostage for years

   b. the three Americans were eventually rescued

   c. the three Americans were hired to do airborne surveillance

4. Choose from the letters below to correctly complete the following statement. Write the letters on the lines.

   According to the article, the purpose of the proof-of-life videos was to _____, which would cause _____, and the effect would be _____.

   a. the hostages would be released

   b. show that the hostages were still alive

   c. the U.S. government or hostage family to pay a ransom

5. From what the article told about the secret agents' mission to free the hostages from the FARC rebels, you can conclude that the American hostages

☐ a. helped the secret agents form the plan that would end by escaping in a helicopter.

☐ b. knew all along about the Colombian secret agents and their plans to rescue them.

☐ c. were never aware that they were about to be rescued until the agents attacked the FARC guards.

---

\_\_\_\_\_ Number of correct answers

Record your personal assessment of your work on the Critical Thinking Chart on page 150.

---

## Personal Response

What was most surprising or interesting to you about this article?

_____

_____

_____

_____

_____

_____

## Self-Assessment

When reading the article, I was having trouble with

_____

_____

_____

_____

_____

_____

_____

_____

_____

_____

_____

_____

_____

_____

_____

# The Lost Boys of Sudan

*Thousands of "Lost Boys," some as young as six years old, crossed from Sudan to Ethiopia and then back again.*

They are often called "The Lost Boys of Sudan," a name that doesn't come close to describing the horrors these children endured. The name was given to them by aid workers because, like the Lost Boys in *Peter Pan*, these children had no parents looking out for them. But while the Lost Boys in *Peter Pan* had a grand time fighting off pirates and crocodiles, the Lost Boys of Sudan spent years struggling through an unrelenting nightmare of homelessness, near starvation, and mass murder.

2    Sudan, the largest country in Africa, has been wracked by an on-again-off-again civil war since 1955, when the southern half of Sudan was united with the northern half. The fighting has been fueled largely by religious and cultural differences. The north is populated primarily by Muslims who consider themselves culturally Arabic, while the south is populated mostly by black Christians who view their culture as more Westernized. After an uneasy cease-fire, fierce fighting broke out again in 1983 when northern forces attacked the south. Since then, the civil war has driven approximately 5 million Sudanese from their homes and has left an estimated 2 million people dead from war-related causes. Caught in the crossfire are thousands of innocent children who have experienced unbelievable grief and hardship.

3    The Lost Boys' terrifying journey started in 1987, when northern forces began bombing and burning hundreds of villages in the south. The invaders slaughtered or enslaved most of the southerners they encountered. Some Lost Boys, many as young as five or six years old, escaped death only because they were out in the fields tending their families' animals when the attacks began. Others survived because their parents told them to flee into the bush as the invaders approached. Five-year-old Alephonsion Deng described what happened as he and two young friends hid in the high grass near his village of Juol.

> Grass roofs lit up like a cluster of torches. Guns started popping. . . . I sobbed as we spent most of the night watching the explosions, until the cries and the fires died away.

4    Frightened and confused, Alephonsion and other young survivors returned to their villages to find their homes destroyed and their parents missing. With nowhere to turn, they began walking toward Ethiopia hundreds of miles away, hoping to find safety there. Some girls also were part of this journey, but a greater number were boys, which is how the term by which the world later came to know them gained support.

5    What began as a stream of young refugees filing toward Ethiopia soon swelled into a river of about 27,000. As they crossed deserts and savannas, many died from starvation, lack of water, or disease. Many others were killed by wild animals such as lions and hyenas. Alephonsion Deng's brother Benson, then seven years old, later described what this miserable two-month journey was like. (Benson and Alephonsion were not traveling together. They had become separated during the attack on their village, and for years neither knew the other was alive.) Each day, wrote Benson, the hot sun beat down without mercy.

> By midday we walked like sick dogs, our steps zigzagging down the road.... My skin was crusty with dirt and sand from sleeping on the ground without a blanket.....

*Benson Deng, Alephonsion Deng, and Benjamin Ajak wrote a book about their journey and their escape to the United States.*

The best estimate is that only about half of the boys who set out on this journey made it to Ethiopia. Among them was Alephonsion's five-year-old cousin Benjamin Ajak, who later wrote:

*I made myself strong like an elder. I made my heart strong. I told myself I was going to make it.*

6    The Lost Boys remained in Ethiopia for more than three years in a variety of refugee camps. Then, in 1991, civil war broke out in Ethiopia, and the boys were ordered out of the country at gunpoint. The children were forced to swim across the crocodile-infested Gilo River back into Sudan. With Ethiopian soldiers firing at their backs, many thousands of boys frantically tried to cross the swirling, swiftly moving river. Benson Deng will never forget it:

*I have many bad memories that I will never erase from my brain, but witnessing how the River Gilo gulped Sudanese underneath to their deathbed will always prevail. . . . People flowed into the river and disappeared like water into the sand of Sahara.*

7    Roughly two thousand boys drowned in the river, were shot, or were devoured by crocodiles. Many who survived literally had to fight their way over or around the mounting corpses. Soon there were so many dead bodies in the water that survivors could not advance without stepping on them, so that some children crossed the river without ever touching the water.

8    Those who survived at Gilo still had to walk hundreds of miles over mountains and through deserts to reach the border of Kenya. With no food or water, the Lost Boys had to scavenge for whatever food they could find while dodging bombing raids by Sudanese soldiers. Despite the grueling and dangerous conditions, the boys clung to the hope that their lives would someday improve. Amazingly, a few of the older boys—ones who had been old enough to attend school before their villages were attacked—had actually managed to carry their school books with them throughout their long journey. Alephonsion recalls some of these boys gathering the younger ones together to read to them.

*Reading made us feel good. As we learned a few things, we saw that in order to understand the world, we needed to be educated. We needed to know about the world around us.*

9    By 1991 some Lost Boys did begin arriving in Kenya. They made it to a refugee center called Kakuma. This was a remote and barren wasteland near the border, but it was the safest place the children had known since being driven from their homes. In the spring of 1992, Benjamin Ajak arrived there, as did Benson and Alephonsion Deng, who had somehow found each other during the long trek from Ethiopia.

10    For some, Kakuma was the end of the road, as many Lost Boys—now grown men—still live in the 10 miles of mud huts and cardboard houses that make up the refugee center. Others were lucky enough to be chosen by relief agencies for relocation to the United States. In 2001 Benson Deng, Alephonsion Deng, and Benjamin Ajak came to live in California, where they co-authored a book about their experiences titled *They Poured Fire on Us from the Sky: The True Story of Three Lost Boys from Sudan.* Somehow they have managed to accept their horrific past and look toward the future. In 2008, during a talk at a local high school, Benjamin Ajak reflected back on his life with these remarkable words:

*I'm a survivor. There's nothing left to be but happy.* ✳

---

*If you have been timed while reading this article, enter your reading time below. Then turn to the Words-per-Minute Table on page 147 and look up your reading speed (words per minute). Enter your reading speed on the graph on page 148.*

**Reading Time: Lesson 12**

_____ : _____

*Minutes*        *Seconds*

# A Finding the Main Idea

One statement below expresses the main idea of the article. One statement is too general, or too broad. The other statement explains only part of the article; it is too narrow. Label the statements using the following key:

**M—Main Idea**       **B—Too Broad**       **N—Too Narrow**

_____ 1. Over the last few decades, civil wars in Sudan have caused incredible danger, hardship, and sorrow for thousands of innocent children.

_____ 2. Although childhood is often thought to be carefree, some children have unbelievably difficult lives.

_____ 3. When forces from northern Sudan bombed and burned villages in southern Sudan in 1987, some children survived because they had been tending animals in the fields that day.

_____ Score 15 points for a correct M answer.

_____ Score 5 points for each correct B or N answer.

_____ **Total Score**: Finding the Main Idea

# B Recalling Facts

How well do you remember the facts in the article? Put an X in the box next to the answer that correctly completes each statement about the article.

1. Most people in the southern half of Sudan are
   - ☐ a. Muslims.
   - ☐ b. Christians.
   - ☐ c. Buddhists.

2. When northern forces destroyed their villages and killed their parents in 1987, many Lost Boys
   - ☐ a. began a long journey on foot to Ethiopia.
   - ☐ b. organized volunteer military units.
   - ☐ c. asked the United Nations for help.

3. After three years in Ethiopia, the Lost Boys
   - ☐ a. were adopted by Ethiopian families.
   - ☐ b. decided that they preferred to live in Sudan.
   - ☐ c. were ordered to leave Ethiopia.

4. Kakuma, Kenya, where many Lost Boys still live, is a
   - ☐ a. barren wasteland.
   - ☐ b. modern city.
   - ☐ c. small town with green farmland.

5. Lost Boy Benjamin Ajak was relocated to
   - ☐ a. South Africa.
   - ☐ b. the United States.
   - ☐ c. Ethiopia.

Score 5 points for each correct answer.

_____ **Total Score**: Recalling Facts

## C Making Inferences

When you combine your own experiences and information from a text to draw a conclusion that is not directly stated in that text, you are making an inference. Below are five statements that may or may not be inferences based on information in the article. Label the statements using the following key:

**C—Correct Inference**          **F—Faulty Inference**

_____ 1. The government of Sudan feels a strong responsibility to protect innocent children.

_____ 2. The Lost Boys have shown that even young children can show courage and strength.

_____ 3. The northern forces were concerned that the Lost Boys would take up weapons against them.

_____ 4. Even the non-desert areas that the Lost Boys traveled across lacked food because so many farms there had been attacked and destroyed.

_____ 5. When the Lost Boys set out for Ethiopia, they knew how far they would have to walk.

---

Score 5 points for each correct answer.

_____ **Total Score**: Making Inferences

---

## D Using Words Precisely

Each numbered sentence below contains an underlined word or phrase from the article. Following the sentence are three definitions. One definition is closest to the meaning of the underlined word. One definition is opposite or nearly opposite. Label those two definitions using the following key. Do not label the remaining definition.

**C—Closest**          **O—Opposite or Nearly Opposite**

1. The Lost Boys of Sudan spent years struggling through an <u>unrelenting</u> nightmare of homelessness, near starvation, and mass murder.

_____ a. never easing up

_____ b. remarkable

_____ c. becoming gradually less difficult

2. What began as a stream of young <u>refugees</u> filing toward Ethiopia soon swelled into a river of about 27,000.

_____ a. people who never leave their own country

_____ b. people who seek safety in a foreign country

_____ c. people who love their country

3. The children were forced to swim across the crocodile-<u>infested</u> Gilo River back into Sudan.

_____ a. very few, in short supply

_____ b. sickening

_____ c. overrun, crowded with

4. "I have many bad memories that I will never erase from my brain, but witnessing how the River Gilo gulped Sudanese underneath to their deathbed will always <u>prevail</u>."

_____ a. change

_____ b. be the strongest

_____ c. go away or fall short

5. With no food or water, the Lost Boys had to <u>scavenge</u> for whatever food they could find while dodging bombing raids by Sudanese soldiers.

_____ a. search

_____ b. throw away

_____ c. prepare

_____ Score 3 points for each correct C answer.

_____ Score 2 points for each correct O answer.

_____ **Total Score**: Using Words Precisely

Enter the four total scores in the spaces below, and add them together to find your Reading Comprehension Score. Then record your score on the graph on page 149.

| Score | Question Type | Lesson 12 |
|---|---|---|
| _____ | Finding the Main Idea | |
| _____ | Recalling Facts | |
| _____ | Making Inferences | |
| _____ | Using Words Precisely | |
| _____ | **Reading Comprehension Score** | |

## Author's Approach

Put an X in the box next to the correct answer.

1. What is the author's purpose in writing this article?
☐ a. to present a critical view of Sudan
☐ b. to inform the reader about the spirit of determination the Lost Boys showed in spite of their suffering
☐ c. to describe what happens when people go to war

2. From the statements below, choose the one that you believe the authors would agree with.
☐ a. The Lost Boys were at least partly responsible for what happened to them.
☐ b. Most people could have done what the Lost Boys did.
☐ c. The Lost Boys showed an amazing ability to help each other while they were refugees.

3. Which of the following statements from the article best describes the Lost Boys now in California?
☐ a. "Somehow they have managed to accept their horrific past and look toward the future."
☐ b. "Each day, wrote Benson, the hot sun beat down without mercy."
☐ c. "Many who survived literally had to fight their way over or around the mounting corpses."

4. In this article, "For some, Kakuma was the end of the road" means
☐ a. Some Lost Boys hated life in Kakuma.
☐ b. Some Lost Boys died in Kakuma.
☐ c. Some Lost Boys still live in Kakuma.

_____ Number of correct answers

Record your personal assessment of your work on the Critical Thinking Chart on page 150.

**CRITICAL THINKING**

## Summarizing and Paraphrasing

Follow the directions provided for questions 1 and 3. Put an X in the box next to the correct answer for question 2.

1. Complete the following one-sentence summary of the article using the lettered phrases from the phrase bank below. Write the letters on the lines.

> **Phrase Bank:**
> a. the hardships the Lost Boys went through
> b. how some of the Lost Boys live today
> c. the events that produced the group called the Lost Boys

The article, "The Lost Boys of Sudan" begins with _____, goes on to describe _____, and ends by describing _____.

2. Choose the sentence that correctly restates the following sentence from the article: "The fighting has been fueled largely by religious and cultural differences."

☐ a. Religious and cultural differences always cause wars.

☐ b. Differences in religion and culture have been the major causes of the fighting.

☐ c. Because there are religious and cultural differences, avoiding conflict has been impossible.

3. Reread paragraph 8 in the article. Below, write a summary of the paragraph in no more than 25 words.

_____

_____

_____

Reread your summary and decide whether it covers the important ideas in the paragraph. Next, decide how to shorten the summary to 15 words or less without leaving out any essential information. Write this summary below.

_____

_____

_____

_____ Number of correct answers

Record your personal assessment of your work on the Critical Thinking Chart on page 150.

## Critical Thinking

Put an X in the box next to the correct answer for questions 1, 3, and 4. Follow the directions provided for the other questions.

1. From the article, you can predict that the Lost Boys will

☐ a. understand that the people who harmed them simply had no choice.

☐ b. have a hard time forgetting the way they were treated.

☐ c. receive money from Sudan to make up for their hardships.

2. Using what you know about the Lost Boys of Sudan and what is told about the Lost Boys in *Peter Pan* in the article, name one way the Lost Boys of Sudan are similar to the Lost Boys in *Peter Pan* and one way they are different. Cite the paragraph number where you found details in the article to support your conclusion.

Similarity

_____

_____

**CRITICAL THINKING**

Difference

_____

_____

_____

3. What was the effect of the outbreak of civil war in Ethiopia?

☐ a. The Ethiopian government blamed the Lost Boys for starting the war.

☐ b. The Ethiopian army burned the refugee village where the Lost Boys were staying.

☐ c. The Lost Boys were forced to leave the country at gunpoint.

4. Judging by events in the article, you can conclude that

☐ a. terrible things happen during wars.

☐ b. even if they are at war, people all over the world understand that children must be protected.

☐ c. sacrifices must be made in order to win a war, but those sacrifices are worth making.

5. In which paragraph did you find your information or details to answer question 3?

_____

_____ Number of correct answers

Record your personal assessment of your work on the Critical Thinking Chart on page 150.

## Personal Response

Why do you think only some of the Lost Boys were chosen to go to the United States?

_____

_____

_____

_____

## Self-Assessment

I really can't understand how

_____

_____

_____

_____

_____

_____

_____

CRITICAL THINKING

# Sudden Attack

*The guided-missile destroyer USS Cole was attacked without warning as it stopped for fuel.*

On the morning of October 12, 2000, the United States Navy destroyer USS *Cole* needed refueling. The 8400-ton ship coasted into the Yemen port of Aden on the southwest coast of the Arabian Peninsula and moved in close to a floating fuel dock. It was 10:30 A.M., and everyone on board expected they would soon be on their way to the Persian Gulf to join the Navy's Fifth Fleet. Some of the *Cole*'s 284 crewmembers were lined up for lunch at the ship's mess hall below deck, and others attended to their various duties around the ship. Out on the water, several small harbor boats maneuvered to assist in attaching the *Cole*'s cable lines to fixed buoys. Gunners Mate Second Class Erin Long was overseeing the procedure near the stern of the ship. "It was creepy," she said. "There were ships everywhere, strewn out sporadically—cargo ships, yachts, old warships—they were all just abandoned. Some were floating on their sides. We had to maneuver between them to get through the harbor."

2    Shortly after 11 A.M., a small boat piloted by two men slowly approached the *Cole*. The men inside waved to the ship in a friendly way. Then, seconds later, the men and the boat disappeared in a fiery blast that ripped a 60-by-40-foot gash in the side of the *Cole*.

3    As seawater rushed into the gaping hole, the destroyer tilted dangerously to the port (left) side. The powerful force of the discharge pushed one of the ship's decks upward and severely damaged the engine room and a mess hall and galley area. The explosion knocked out the *Cole*'s internal communication system as well as most of its electricity. The entire crew was plunged into chaos that consisted of darkness, heat, and thick smoke. Sailors were knocked off their feet and showered with soot and oil from broken fuel tanks. Bloodied bodies lay everywhere—some dead, others unconscious, and still others pinned down by twisted metal from the ship's deck and bulkheads. No one inside the ship knew what had caused the explosion. If it was an attack, it was anyone's guess whether they would be attacked again.

4    For the crew members who could move and were not injured, the first order of business was to save lives. A few sailors, finding themselves isolated from their chain of command, began to take charge and give orders. One of these was Hospital Corpsman Third Class Tayinikia Campbell, who was down in the sick bay on the starboard (right) side of the ship when the attack occurred. In the aftermath, she heard people in the corridors shouting "Get out! Get out!" and calling for medical help. Campbell's training included only first aid and basic medical care in a combat situation, but she rushed out of the smoke-filled sick bay and shouted back a hopeful response, "I'm right here!"

5    Working in a darkened passageway with Seaman Eben Sanchez, Campbell quickly set up an improvised triage area. Although some sailors began carrying injured sailors to this area, others, said Campbell, "were just sitting there, freaking out." She managed to calm these sailors down by giving them basic jobs to carry out, such as collecting supplies. Everywhere she looked, injured

*Hospital Corpsman Third Class Tayinikia Campbell and others acted quickly to help the injured.*

sailors with broken legs, facial cuts, and crushed limbs were moaning for help. The *Cole* was not a large enough ship to have its own doctor on board, so in these extreme circumstances, there was no one else to help. Command Master Chief James Parlier joined Campbell and Sanchez in preparing to help the wounded in the triage area. The three spent the next 90 minutes treating the injured and arranging to get them off the ship to a hospital. Working under the dim light of battle lanterns, they treated the most serious injuries as best they could.

6    Meanwhile, the ship's commanders had gotten hold of a few hand-held radios and began to communicate with each other from different areas of the ship. They sent their orders to security teams via handwritten messages carried by runners.

7    It would be hours before help could arrive, so it was up to the able-bodied men and women to form teams to find and rescue their stricken shipmates. One rescue party heard screams in a second mess area close to the center of the blast. "There are people in there!" someone yelled. The bulkhead door to the mess hall was blocked, so uninjured crewmembers used their hands and feet and whatever tools they could grab to pound their way in. Once inside, the team was forced to make quick life-and-death decisions about who they could actually help. If an injured sailor didn't respond, they moved on to the next

one. They carried those who were still alive to the passageway where Campbell and Sanchez were working.

8    Meanwhile, one deck below the mess hall, the explosion had torn into another room, completely cutting it off from the rest of the ship and trapping three crewmembers inside it. One of those trapped sailors was Technician First Class Margaret Lopez, who suffered serious burns on more than 20 percent of her body. With water surging into the room through the hole in the side of the *Cole*, Lopez knew she had to act. Despite her injuries, she waded through waist-deep water and heavy oil and guided one of her fellow sailors through the hole and out into the sea. The sailor swam to the surface as Lopez headed back into the ship to search for the other person she knew had been in the room, Ensign Andrew Triplett. Unable to find Triplett amid the wreckage, Lopez swam back outside and then up and down the side of the *Cole*. Her search was in vain. Sailors still on board eventually lifted her out of the sea, along with the sailor she had rescued. Lopez later learned that Ensign Triplett had died in the blast.

9    Eventually it was determined that the waving men in the small boat were terrorists. Their cargo contained hundreds of pounds of explosives, which they hoped would be enough to sink or destroy the USS *Cole*. The ship did not sink, though, despite the terrible damage to its hull.

10    Fourteen months later, after extensive repairs, the USS *Cole* returned to active duty. The newly repaired vessel set sail with 550 tons of new steel, improved security, and a crew that included 40 sailors who had survived the October 12 attack. There was one other new feature also—a collection of 17 stars embedded in a hallway floor, one for each sailor killed in the attack. Tayinikia Campbell, Eben Sanchez, James Parlier, Margaret Lopez, and others showed the world a classic example of U.S. military teamwork and bravery under fire. Without their heroic actions, there would have been many more stars laid down in memorial. ✵

*If you have been timed while reading this article, enter your reading time below. Then turn to the Words-per-Minute Table on page 147 and look up your reading speed (words per minute). Enter your reading speed on the graph on page 148.*

**Reading Time: Lesson 13**

_____ : _____
  *Minutes*          *Seconds*

## A Finding the Main Idea

One statement below expresses the main idea of the article. One statement is too general, or too broad. The other statement explains only part of the article; it is too narrow. Label the statements using the following key:

**M—Main Idea**　　　**B—Too Broad**　　　**N—Too Narrow**

_____ 1. Members of the armed forces must always be aware that they might be attacked by terrorists.

_____ 2. Crewmembers of the USS *Cole* responded bravely after a surprise terrorist attack.

_____ 3. After the terrorist attack on the USS *Cole*, some crewmembers set up teams to locate the injured and to take them to the triage area for treatment.

_____ Score 15 points for a correct M answer.

_____ Score 5 points for each correct B or N answer.

_____ **Total Score**: Finding the Main Idea

## B Recalling Facts

How well do you remember the facts in the article? Put an X in the box next to the answer that correctly completes each statement about the article.

1. The USS *Cole* was
   - ☐ a. an aircraft carrier.
   - ☐ b. a submarine.
   - ☐ c. a destroyer.

2. On the day of the attack, the USS *Cole* was going to
   - ☐ a. the Persian Gulf.
   - ☐ b. the Mediterranean Sea.
   - ☐ c. the Black Sea.

3. Tayinikia Campbell and Eben Sanchez helped by
   - ☐ a. finding hand-held radios so commanders could communicate.
   - ☐ b. setting up a triage area to treat the wounded.
   - ☐ c. searching the ship for injured crewmembers.

4. Hours before help arrived, crewmembers
   - ☐ a. reported to their commanders for orders.
   - ☐ b. tried to find the cause of the explosion.
   - ☐ c. formed search-and-rescue teams.

5. The sailors killed in the attack are memorialized by
   - ☐ a. stars embedded in a floor on the repaired *Cole*.
   - ☐ b. stars on the flag that the *Cole* now flies.
   - ☐ c. armbands that the *Cole* crewmembers wear.

Score 5 points for each correct answer.

_____ **Total Score**: Recalling Facts

## C Making Inferences

When you combine your own experiences and information from a text to draw a conclusion that is not directly stated in that text, you are making an inference. Below are five statements that may or may not be inferences based on information in the article. Label the statements using the following key:

**C—Correct Inference**          **F—Faulty Inference**

_____ 1. The fueling port in the Gulf of Aden was poorly organized and not very secure.

_____ 2. You can always identify terrorists by the way they look, even before they commit their acts of terrorism.

_____ 3. The crewmembers on the USS *Cole* were very nervous before the attack.

_____ 4. Without artificial lights, the passageways on a large ship are dark even on a bright day.

_____ 5. Margaret Lopez guided the sailor through the hole in the ship and out into the sea because it was the quickest route to safety.

---

Score 5 points for each correct answer.

_____ **Total Score**: Making Inferences

---

## D Using Words Precisely

Each numbered sentence below contains an underlined word or phrase from the article. Following the sentence are three definitions. One definition is closest to the meaning of the underlined word. One definition is opposite or nearly opposite. Label those two definitions using the following key. Do not label the remaining definition.

**C—Closest**          **O—Opposite or Nearly Opposite**

1. "There were ships everywhere, strewn out <u>sporadically</u>—cargo ships, yachts, old warships—they were all just abandoned."

   _____ a. in a regular arrangement

   _____ b. widely, over a large area

   _____ c. with no apparent pattern

2. In the <u>aftermath</u>, she heard people in the corridors shouting "Get out! Get out!" and calling for medical help.

   _____ a. time before an event

   _____ b. period following an event

   _____ c. exciting period of time

3. Working in a darkened passageway with Seaman Eben Sanchez, Campbell quickly set up an <u>improvised</u> triage area.

   _____ a. filled with hope

   _____ b. made quickly, with little preparation

   _____ c. created according to a well-thought-out plan

4. It was up to the able-bodied men and women to form teams to find and rescue their <u>stricken</u> shipmates.

   _____ a. weakened or wounded

   _____ b. out of the way

   _____ c. healthy and strong

5. Fourteen months later, after <u>extensive</u> repairs, the USS *Cole* returned to active duty.

_____ a. great in degree or amount

_____ b. hardly noticeable

_____ c. very expensive

_____ Score 3 points for each correct C answer.

_____ Score 2 points for each correct O answer.

_____ **Total Score**: Using Words Precisely

Enter the four total scores in the spaces below, and add them together to find your Reading Comprehension Score. Then record your score on the graph on page 149.

| Score | Question Type | Lesson 13 |
|---|---|---|
| _____ | Finding the Main Idea | |
| _____ | Recalling Facts | |
| _____ | Making Inferences | |
| _____ | Using Words Precisely | |
| _____ | **Reading Comprehension Score** | |

## Author's Approach

Put an X in the box next to the correct answer.

1. The main purpose of the first paragraph is to
   ☐ a. let the reader know where the USS *Cole* was and what it was doing before the attack.
   ☐ b. describe the duties of sailors aboard the USS *Cole*.
   ☐ c. tell how many sailors were aboard the USS *Cole*.

2. From the statements below, choose the one that you believe the author would agree with.
   ☐ a. All of the sailors should have survived the blast, no matter how powerful it was.
   ☐ b. The crewmembers of the USS *Cole* tried hard to rescue and treat their fellow sailors after the explosion.
   ☐ c. The officers on the USS *Cole* were fairly certain that an attack was coming that day.

3. How is the author's purpose for writing the article expressed in paragraph 10?
   ☐ a. This paragraph stresses that 40 sailors who survived the attack were part of the new crew.
   ☐ b. This paragraph explains why a memorial was placed in the repaired USS *Cole*.
   ☐ c. This paragraph states that the crewmembers of the USS *Cole* showed excellent teamwork and bravery.

_____ Number of correct answers

Record your personal assessment of your work on the Critical Thinking Chart on page 150.

# Summarizing and Paraphrasing

Follow the directions provided for questions 1 and 2. Put an X in the box next to the correct answer for question 3.

1.  Complete the following one-sentence summary of the article using the lettered phrases from the phrase bank below. Write the letters on the lines.

---

**Phrase Bank:**

a.  what happened to the ship and its crew after the attack

b.  how the crewmembers responded to the attack

c.  a description of what was happening before the attack

---

The article "Sudden Attack" begins with _____, goes on to describe _____, and ends with _____.

2.  Look for the important ideas and events in paragraph 5. Summarize the paragraph in one or two sentences.

_____

_____

_____

_____

_____

_____

_____

_____

_____

_____

3.  Choose the sentence that correctly restates the following sentence from the article: "She managed to calm these sailors down by giving them basic jobs to carry out, such as collecting supplies."

☐ a.  She calmed the sailors down by performing basic jobs, such as collecting supplies.

☐ b.  She gave the sailors basic jobs, such as collecting supplies, in order to calm them down.

☐ c.  When the sailors calmed down, she gave them a few basic jobs to carry out, including collecting supplies.

---

_____ Number of correct answers

Record your personal assessment of your work on the Critical Thinking Chart on page 150.

---

# Critical Thinking

Put an X in the box next to the correct answer for questions 1 and 4. Follow the directions provided for the other questions.

1.  Which of the following statements from the article is an opinion rather than a fact?

☐ a.  "Lopez later learned that Ensign Triplett had died in the blast."

☐ b.  "Tayinikia Campbell, Eben Sanchez, James Parlier, Margaret Lopez, and others demonstrated to the world a classic example of U.S. military teamwork and bravery under fire."

☐ c.  "The three spent the next 90 minutes treating the injured and arranging to get them off the ship to a hospital."

2. Choose from the letters below to correctly complete the following statement. Write the letters on the lines.

   In the article, _____ and _____ are different because one treated the wounds of the sailors, while the other one searched for the wounded.

   a. Tayinikia Campbell

   b. Andrew Triplett

   c. Margaret Lopez

3. Reread paragraph 5. Then choose from the letters below to correctly complete the following statement. Write the letters on the lines.

   According to paragraph 5, _____ because _____.

   a. the terrorist attack came as a complete surprise

   b. the USS *Cole* had no doctor on board

   c. the USS *Cole* was a relatively small ship

4. What did you have to do to answer question 2?

   ☐ a. find an opinion (what someone thinks about something)

   ☐ b. find a contrast (how things are different)

   ☐ c. draw a conclusion (a sensible statement based on the text and your experience)

   _____ Number of correct answers

   Record your personal assessment of your work on the Critical Thinking Chart on page 150.

## Personal Response

A question I would like answered by Technician First Class Margaret Lopez is

_____

_____

_____

_____

## Self-Assessment

Before reading this article, I already knew

_____

_____

_____

_____

_____

_____

_____

_____

_____

CRITICAL THINKING

# Snowbound

*Warning signs in the road should have been enough to persuade the Garners not to enter Modena Canyon.*

It all started because Tom and Tamitha Garner wanted some pictures of wild horses. The couple was on a trip through Iron County in southern Utah and was hoping to snap a few photos of the mustangs that roamed freely in this remote section of the state. So on January 26, 2008, Tom and his wife, Tamitha, accompanied by their dog, a mixed-breed named Medusa, turned off Route 56 and headed up an isolated dirt road into the mountains. Bouncing along in their gray pickup truck, they entered Modena Canyon, where they noticed warning signs urging motorists to travel no farther. The signs made them pause, but then they saw a car coming out of the canyon driven by an elderly woman. They figured that if she could navigate this narrow, winding back road, so could they. As Tom Garner later said, "I thought, 'How bad could it be?'"

2 The answer to that question came soon enough. At first, there had been a dusting of snow on the road, but then the snow began to accumulate and get deeper, with bigger and bigger drifts blown across the road. After about 20 miles, the Garners found the horses they were looking for and happily took pictures until the herd ran off. Excited, they followed the horses farther into the canyon, but kept getting stuck in the snow. Again and again, Tom used a small shovel from the truck to free the wheels. Finally, however, they plowed into a drift so deep they could not go forward or backward. By this time, night was settling in, so the Garners decided the smart thing

to do was to spend the night in their truck and dig themselves out in the morning, when they would be able to see what they were doing. They tried to call their 19-year-old daughter Krystal on their cell phones, but they could not get a signal.

3 Unfortunately, as the couple and the dog huddled together under blankets in their truck that night, the snowfall turned into a blizzard. The winds kicked up to 50 miles per hour, and the temperature dropped to five degrees below zero. By daylight, the entire area was blanketed with

deep snow, and the Garners' truck was half-buried under a giant drift. Tom tried to dig the truck out, but he found the task impossible. Wearing only sneakers and an unlined jacket, he quickly became chilled and had to climb back inside. Meanwhile, the snow continued to swirl, blowing 6-foot drifts around the vehicle. Both Tom and Tamitha realized they had no hope of driving out of the canyon.

4 The Garners considered trying to walk back toward Route 56, but with so much fresh snow covering the canyon, it would

*The Garners and their dog were stranded for 12 days when their truck became stuck in the snow.*

be easy to wander off course. Besides, Tom knew that they would never be able to cover the 20-odd miles in sneakers without freezing their feet. "We might make it," he said, "but we'd lose our feet to frostbite and spend the rest of our lives in wheelchairs." Instead, they decided to sit tight and wait for rescuers to find them.

5    For the next eight days, the couple remained in their truck. They rationed their food, which consisted of a couple of boxes of granola bars, some bottled water, one jar of peanut butter and another of jam, plus dog food for Medusa. They ran the truck engine sparingly, turning it on only when they really needed to warm up. The rest of the time, they huddled together in the cold. "It was brutal," Tamitha later said. By 6:30 each night the windows were frozen shut, and every day brought more snow, with the sky only occasionally clearing enough for them to see patches of blue. The Garners heard the sound of a few search planes overhead, but none came very close, and with their gray truck covered with snow, they weren't particularly visible anyway. Tom used the mirror from the visor to flash sunlight up at the planes, but none of the pilots spotted his signal. At one point, fearing she would not survive, Tamitha found a scrap of paper and wrote a goodbye note to Krystal. Later, Tom wrote a similar note.

6    Finally, on the ninth day, the Garners decided their only hope was to leave the truck and try to make it back to civilization on foot. By now, they were nearly out of food and water and had been reduced to eating Medusa's dog food. Tom remembered seeing a TV show where someone had made snowshoes out of seat cushions. So, copying that idea, he cut foam cubes from the seat of the truck and used bungee cords to attach them to his and Tamitha's feet. Then they gathered a few things they thought might come in handy—a cigarette lighter, a spray can of deodorant, a couple of umbrellas— and threw them into a garbage bag. Snowdrifts prevented them from opening the truck doors, but they managed to crawl out of the truck window, pull out their gear, and begin walking, with Medusa bounding in their tracks.

7    Although the makeshift snowshoes worked well for Tom, Tamitha had less luck. The snowshoes kept slipping off her feet, so finally she abandoned them altogether. In an effort to keep Tamitha's sneakers dry, Tom began walking sideways ahead of her, packing down the snow to form a trail for her to walk in. By late afternoon, they were both exhausted. They stopped under a tree to set up camp for the night and used the open umbrellas as shields against the wind. Then they collected some twigs, sprayed deodorant on them, and used the lighter to start a fire.

8    On Tuesday the sky was sunny and the temperature warmed up to above freezing, but the snow turned slushy, which made traveling more difficult. Because of their poor night's sleep and their weariness from the previous day's exertion, the Garners began to struggle. Throughout the day, they encouraged each other to continue moving and then spent a second night huddled around an open-air fire. This time they were worried about the coyotes that had started to howl as they made their camp. They hoped the fire and the presence of Medusa would be enough to keep the coyotes away.

9    By Wednesday morning, Tamitha was almost delirious; she thought she heard people laughing and smelled cookies baking. Then she thought she heard a truck engine, which, in fact, turned out to be real, and was growing louder. Rounding a bend in the distance, the Garners witnessed a road grader clearing a trail through the snow. The couple staggered toward it, shouting at the driver and waving their arms. When the truck slowed down, they knew they were saved at last. They had survived 12 horrific days snowbound in the wilderness. ✳

*If you have been timed while reading this article, enter your reading time below. Then turn to the Words-per-Minute Table on page 147 and look up your reading speed (words per minute). Enter your reading speed on the graph on page 148.*

**Reading Time: Lesson 14**

_____ : _____

*Minutes          Seconds*

## A | Finding the Main Idea

One statement below expresses the main idea of the article. One statement is too general, or too broad. The other statement explains only part of the article; it is too narrow. Label the statements using the following key:

**M—Main Idea**      **B—Too Broad**      **N—Too Narrow**

_____ 1. Tom and Tamitha Garner wanted to take pictures in a canyon in south Utah, so they drove down a remote dirt road in their gray pickup truck.

_____ 2. A couple who drove into a mountain canyon became snowbound but survived for 12 days on their own in the wilderness.

_____ 3. Mountain wilderness areas can turn dangerous when blizzards hit, as one couple found out.

_____ Score 15 points for a correct M answer.

_____ Score 5 points for each correct B or N answer.

_____ **Total Score**: Finding the Main Idea

## B | Recalling Facts

How well do you remember the facts in the article? Put an X in the box next to the answer that correctly completes each statement about the article.

1. The Garners hoped to get some photographs of
   - ☐ a. the moon over the mountains.
   - ☐ b. Modena Canyon in the snow.
   - ☐ c. wild horses that live in Modena Canyon.

2. The Garners stayed overnight in their truck because
   - ☐ a. they wanted to take more pictures in the morning.
   - ☐ b. their car was stuck in a snowdrift.
   - ☐ c. they were tired of driving.

3. Fearing they would not survive, Tom and Tamitha wrote goodbye notes to their
   - ☐ a. daughter.
   - ☐ b. lawyer.
   - ☐ c. parents.

4. The Garners used the truck's seat cushions as
   - ☐ a. snowshoes.
   - ☐ b. shields against the wind.
   - ☐ c. fuel for campfires.

5. The Garners were finally rescued by
   - ☐ a. a hiker in snowshoes.
   - ☐ b. the driver of a road grader.
   - ☐ c. an emergency helicopter.

Score 5 points for each correct answer.

_____ **Total Score**: Recalling Facts

# C Making Inferences

When you combine your own experiences and information from a text to draw a conclusion that is not directly stated in that text, you are making an inference. Below are five statements that may or may not be inferences based on information in the article. Label the statements using the following key:

**C—Correct Inference**       **F—Faulty Inference**

_____ 1. You cannot count on cell phones to work in every location.

_____ 2. If the Garners had sent their dog out for help they would have been rescued sooner.

_____ 3. The Garners were glad they had brought their dog for the extra body heat it supplied.

_____ 4. Tom and Tamitha had planned their trip with great care.

_____ 5. The Garners survived because they were creative, clever, and calm.

Score 5 points for each correct answer.

_____ **Total Score**: Making Inferences

# D Using Words Precisely

Each numbered sentence below contains an underlined word or phrase from the article. Following the sentence are three definitions. One definition is closest to the meaning of the underlined word. One definition is opposite or nearly opposite. Label those two definitions using the following key. Do not label the remaining definition.

**C—Closest**       **O—Opposite or Nearly Opposite**

1. Soon the snow began to <u>accumulate</u> and get deeper.

_____ a. linger

_____ b. melt

_____ c. build

2. They <u>rationed</u> their food, which consisted of a couple of boxes of granola bars, some bottled water, one jar of peanut butter and another of jam, plus dog food for Medusa.

_____ a. used up completely

_____ b. used only certain amounts

_____ c. kept organized

3. They ran the truck engine <u>sparingly</u>, turning it on only when they really needed to warm up.

_____ a. freely, with excess

_____ b. in a limited amount

_____ c. gratefully

4. Because of their poor night's sleep and their weariness from the previous day's <u>exertion</u>, Tom and Tamitha were struggling.

_____ a. frightening events

_____ b. rest and relaxation

_____ c. difficult physical effort

5. By Wednesday morning, Tamitha was almost <u>delirious</u>; she thought she heard people laughing and smelled cookies baking.

_____ a. extremely confused; not thinking clearly

_____ b. exhausted

_____ c. sensible and realistic

_____ Score 3 points for each correct C answer.

_____ Score 2 points for each correct O answer.

_____ **Total Score**: Using Words Precisely

Enter the four total scores in the spaces below, and add them together to find your Reading Comprehension Score. Then record your score on the graph on page 149.

| Score | Question Type | Lesson 14 |
|---|---|---|
| _____ | Finding the Main Idea | |
| _____ | Recalling Facts | |
| _____ | Making Inferences | |
| _____ | Using Words Precisely | |
| _____ | **Reading Comprehension Score** | |

## Author's Approach

Put an X in the box next to the correct answer.

1. The main purpose of the first paragraph is to
 ☐ a. suggest that the problems the Garners would face were unavoidable.
 ☐ b. identify the characters and setting of the action.
 ☐ c. emphasize that the Garners loved wild horses.

2. What does the author imply by saying "On Tuesday the sky was sunny, and the temperature warmed up to above freezing, but the snow turned slushy, which made traveling more difficult."
 ☐ a. The Garners missed their chance to go back to the truck.
 ☐ b. The weather had changed from very cold to very warm.
 ☐ c. The colder weather had made the snow easier to walk on because it was not slushy, but firm.

3. The author probably wrote this article in order to
 ☐ a. entertain readers with an interesting story of survival.
 ☐ b. persuade readers to stay off mountain roads in winter.
 ☐ c. describe the weather in southern Utah in January.

4. The author tells this story mainly by
 ☐ a. comparing different topics.
 ☐ b. using imagination or creativity.
 ☐ c. describing events in the order they happened.

_____ Number of correct answers

Record your personal assessment of your work on the Critical Thinking Chart on page 150.

# Summarizing and Paraphrasing

Put an X in the box next to the correct answer.

1.  Read the statement about the article below. Then read the paraphrase of that statement. Choose the reason that best tells why the paraphrase does not say the same thing as the statement.

    Statement:   Again and again, Tom used a small shovel from the truck to free the wheels.

    Paraphrase:  Luckily, Tom had brought a small shovel to free the wheels.

    ☐  a.  Paraphrase says too much.

    ☐  b.  Paraphrase doesn't say enough.

    ☐  c.  Paraphrase doesn't agree with the statement.

2.  Below are summaries of the article. Choose the summary that says all the most important things about the article but in the fewest words.

    ☐  a.  Tom and Tamitha Garner and their dog Medusa barely survived being snowbound in a canyon in Utah.

    ☐  b.  Tom and Tamitha Garner wanted to take pictures of wild horses, so they drove down a mountain road in winter. When a blizzard struck, they were trapped in their truck with little to eat and no warm clothes to wear. Days later, they decided to leave the truck and walk to civilization. Luckily, they were rescued.

    ☐  c.  A sudden January blizzard trapped Tom and Tamitha Garner in their truck on an isolated mountain canyon road. They waited there for several days and finally walked to a road where they were rescued.

    _____ Number of correct answers

    Record your personal assessment of your work on the Critical Thinking Chart on page 150.

# Critical Thinking

Follow the directions provided for questions 1, 3, 4, and 5. Put an X in the box next to the correct answer for question 2.

1.  For each statement below, write O if it expresses an opinion or write F if it expresses a fact.

    _____  a.  The Garners should have known not to travel any further into the canyon.

    _____  b.  The Garners were worried about the coyotes they heard as they made camp.

    _____  c.  Tom got the idea for using seat cushions for snowshoes from a TV show.

2.  From the article, you can predict that if the Garners go driving down mountain roads in winter again, they will

    ☐  a.  pack more food and warmer clothes.

    ☐  b.  hike instead of driving a truck.

    ☐  c.  bring a lot more people along.

3.  Choose from the letters below to correctly complete the following statement. Write the letters on the lines.

    On the positive side, _____, but on the negative side, _____.

    a.  the Garners wrote goodbye notes to their daughter

    b.  the Garners had a frightening and miserable 12 days

    c.  the Garners survived

4.  Choose from the letters below to correctly complete the following statement. Write the letters on the lines.

    According to the article, _____ caused the Garners' truck to _____, and the effect was _____.

    a.  become trapped in the snow

    b.  the Garners were snowbound

    c.  a sudden blizzard

5.  Which paragraphs provide evidence that supports your answer to question 4?

_____

---

_____ Number of correct answers

Record your personal assessment of your work on the Critical Thinking Chart on page 150.

---

## Personal Response

What was most surprising or interesting to you about this article?

_____

_____

_____

_____

_____

_____

_____

_____

## Self-Assessment

One of the things I did best when reading this article was

_____

_____

_____

_____

_____

_____

I believe I did this well because

_____

_____

_____

_____

_____

_____

_____

CRITICAL THINKING

# Death Roll in the River

*Australian river crocodiles, which can grow up to 20 feet in length, usually will not attack humans.*

What a difference a day makes! Val Plumwood's journey through Australia's Kakadu National Park had been idyllic and peaceful. It was February 1985, and the 45-year-old Plumwood had been canoeing through the park in search of ancient rock art created by the Aboriginal people. On this second day, a light drizzle moved in, and then quickly turned into a heavy downpour. Plumwood, an author of books about the relationships between organisms and their environment, was not bothered by the cloudburst. She steered her canoe out of the river's main current and into a narrow branch of the river. Paddling along, she spotted what at first appeared to be a large stick floating in the middle of the river. She later recalled, "As the current moved me toward it, the stick developed eyes. It was a crocodile!"

2    At first, Plumwood was more fascinated than frightened, since before the trip everyone had assured her that crocodiles do not attack canoes. So she found it puzzling that when she steered her canoe to go around the crocodile, the creature moved in closer. Still, she was confident she could maneuver past it and continue on her way. She was completely unprepared when the crocodile suddenly struck the canoe. This wasn't supposed to happen—but it *did* happen—the crocodile had attacked her!

3    Plumwood paddled furiously to get away, but the crocodile kept bashing the canoe. Experts later guessed that it was a territorial male that had mistaken the canoe for a rival crocodile. Whatever the reason was, it didn't much concern Plumwood, who realized that she had to get out of the canoe fast. Unfortunately the riverbank in that section of the river was a high, steep, slippery wall of mud, and it didn't appear to offer Plumwood a single possible escape route. Plumwood spotted a tree near the bank with its trunk growing up from under the water, and she quickly decided that leaping up onto one of the tree's branches was her best option. Before abandoning her canoe, Plumwood made one final effort to scare off the crocodile by flailing her arms and trying to look fearsome while shouting, "Go away!" This kind of bluff might have worked with some wild animals, but it had absolutely no effect on this creature. As Plumwood leaped for the branch, the crocodile lunged at her, grabbed her in mid-air by the legs, and pulled her down into the water.

4    The crocodile now had Plumwood in its "death roll." Due to its unique breathing and heart processes, a crocodile is not built for a prolonged struggle with a victim, so it uses

*Val Plumwood viewed her near-fatal experience as a lesson about the relationship between humans and other creatures.*

a "death roll," an intense burst of power designed to destroy its victim's resistance. A crocodile will then hold its prey under water until the prey drowns. Just when Plumwood was certain she was about to die, the crocodile stopped rolling and unclenched its jaws. Plumwood felt her feet touch the bottom of the river, and when she stood up, she realized the river was shallow enough so that her head popped out of the water. Plumwood took a deep, gasping breath, amazed to be still alive—and then the crocodile renewed its grip and sent her down into a second death roll.

5    When the rolling stopped, Plumwood was still conscious, but she feared she wouldn't be for much longer. Frantically, she tried again to climb to safety in the nearby tree. "I grabbed the branch," she later recalled, "vowing to let the crocodile tear me apart rather than throw me again into that spinning, suffocating hell." Once again, however, the crocodile was too quick for her; it latched onto Plumwood's upper left thigh and yanked her down again for a third death roll.

6    Incredibly, Plumwood survived the third roll as well. She was certain that the crocodile would kill her, but she now realized that it "was going to take a long time over it, which seemed worse than having it kill me straight out." Knowing it was useless to try to reach the branch again, Plumwood threw herself against the steep mud bank and attempted to scramble up

onto it. However, the rain had been coming down hard for hours, and the riverbank was slick and muddy. Plumwood managed to climb far enough to escape the crocodile's reach but then started slipping back down. She struggled desperately to climb higher, and several times slid back down perilously close to the crocodile's jaws. At last, she stabbed her fingers deep into the mud and called upon her last reserves of strength to hoist herself up to the top of the bank.

7    Plumwood reached the top and was now safe from the crocodile, but she was all alone, very badly injured, and miles from any help. For hours, Plumwood endured searing pain as she dragged her body through the downpour, trying to get to the nearest park ranger station. Finally, she came to a large swamp that separated her from the station, and her heart sank. She had paddled across this swamp earlier in the day, but without her canoe, she had no way to get back across.

8    Plumwood collapsed exhausted and bleeding at the edge of the swamp. As she later described it, "I lay there in the gathering dusk to await what would come. . . . I doubted I could last the night." Mercifully, the rain stopped and the wind died down. Then Plumwood saw the light of a park ranger's motorbike on the far side of the swamp. She called out to the ranger, who was on patrol, and was lucky enough that her voice carried to him through the night air. Rescuers soon found Plumwood and

scooped her up and transported her for 13 hours to a hospital in Darwin.

9    The doctors managed to save Plumwood's chewed and badly damaged leg and even repaired the skin. Throughout the months-long recovery period, she insisted that park rangers should not seek out and destroy the crocodile that had tried to kill her. "I was intruding into its territory," she told them, "and no good purpose could be served by revenge." In her writings on ecology, Plumwood used her experience with the crocodile to make the point that humans should not think of themselves as "above the food chain." Plumwood said the crocodile's actions helped her to glimpse "a shockingly indifferent world." In nature, she realized, humans had no more importance than any other edible being. ✳

If you have been timed while reading this article, enter your reading time below. Then turn to the Words-per-Minute Table on page 147 and look up your reading speed (words per minute). Enter your reading speed on the graph on page 148.

**Reading Time: Lesson 15**

_____ : _____

*Minutes*          *Seconds*

## A Finding the Main Idea

One statement below expresses the main idea of the article. One statement is too general, or too broad. The other statement explains only part of the article; it is too narrow. Label the statements using the following key:

**M—Main Idea**     **B—Too Broad**     **N—Too Narrow**

_____ 1. Val Plumwood had to struggle to survive after she was attacked by a crocodile while canoeing in Australia.

_____ 2. Visitors to Kakadu National Park in northern Australia may come across crocodiles and other wildlife.

_____ 3. Val Plumwood attempted to escape an attacking crocodile by leaping onto a tree branch.

_____ Score 15 points for a correct M answer.

_____ Score 5 points for each correct B or N answer.

_____ **Total Score**: Finding the Main Idea

## B Recalling Facts

How well do you remember the facts in the article? Put an X in the box next to the answer that correctly completes each statement about the article.

1. When Plumwood first saw the crocodile, she was
   ☐ a. fascinated.
   ☐ b. frightened.
   ☐ c. annoyed.

2. Plumwood tried to scare the crocodile away by
   ☐ a. slapping the water with an oar.
   ☐ b. ramming the crocodile with the canoe.
   ☐ c. waving her arms and shouting.

3. The crocodile pulled Plumwood into a death roll
   ☐ a. twice.
   ☐ b. three times.
   ☐ c. four times.

4. Plumwood could not get to the ranger station because the station was on the other side of a
   ☐ a. dense grove of trees.
   ☐ b. river.
   ☐ c. swamp.

5. After she was rescued, Plumwood told the park rangers to
   ☐ a. trap the crocodile.
   ☐ b. let the crocodile live.
   ☐ c. shoot the crocodile.

Score 5 points for each correct answer.

_____ **Total Score**: Recalling Facts

## C Making Inferences

When you combine your own experiences and information from a text to draw a conclusion that is not directly stated in that text, you are making an inference. Below are five statements that may or may not be inferences based on information in the article. Label the statements using the following key:

**C—Correct Inference**          **F—Faulty Inference**

_____  1.  Crocodiles are rare or seldom seen in that part of Australia.

_____  2.  Plumwood should not have been canoeing alone in an area inhabited by dangerous creatures.

_____  3.  This was not the first time Plumwood had an encounter with a crocodile.

_____  4.  Only scientists like Val Plumwood ever go to Kakadu National Park.

_____  5.  One death roll is usually enough for a crocodile to defeat its prey.

---

Score 5 points for each correct answer.

_____  **Total Score**: Making Inferences

---

## D Using Words Precisely

Each numbered sentence below contains an underlined word or phrase from the article. Following the sentence are three definitions. One definition is closest to the meaning of the underlined word. One definition is opposite or nearly opposite. Label those two definitions using the following key. Do not label the remaining definition.

**C—Closest**          **O—Opposite or Nearly Opposite**

1.  Plumwood made one final effort to scare off the crocodile by <u>flailing</u> her arms and trying to look fearsome while shouting, "Go away!"

_____  a.  flapping, waving

_____  b.  holding rigidly

_____  c.  rubbing

2.  A crocodile is not built for a <u>prolonged</u> struggle with a victim, so it uses a "death roll," a short, intense burst of power designed to kill its victims.

_____  a.  shortened

_____  b.  violent

_____  c.  extended, lengthy

3.  For hours, Plumwood endured <u>searing</u> pain as she dragged her body through the downpour, trying to get to the nearest park ranger station.

_____  a.  sudden

_____  b.  burning

_____  c.  cool

4.  "I was <u>intruding</u> into its territory," she told them, "and no good purpose could be served by revenge."

_____  a.  calling noisily

_____  b.  welcomed

_____  c.  entering without permission or right

5. Plumwood said the crocodile's actions helped her to glimpse "a shockingly <u>indifferent</u> world."

_____ a. caring, concerned

_____ b. unfeeling, uninterested

_____ c. strange, peculiar

---

_____ Score 3 points for each correct C answer.

_____ Score 2 points for each correct O answer.

_____ **Total Score**: Using Words Precisely

---

Enter the four total scores in the spaces below, and add them together to find your Reading Comprehension Score. Then record your score on the graph on page 149.

| Score | Question Type | Lesson 15 |
|---|---|---|
| _____ | Finding the Main Idea | |
| _____ | Recalling Facts | |
| _____ | Making Inferences | |
| _____ | Using Words Precisely | |
| _____ | **Reading Comprehension Score** | |

## Author's Approach

Put an X in the box next to the correct answer.

1. The author probably wrote this article in order to
☐ a. encourage people to take canoe trips in Australia.
☐ b. invite the reader to think of the wild side of nature.
☐ c. persuade the reader to be afraid of wild animals.

2. The author tells this story mainly by
☐ a. using the first-person point of view.
☐ b. repeating statements made by Plumwood.
☐ c. describing events as Plumwood remembered them.

3. Considering the statement from the article "Throughout the months-long recovery period, she insisted that park rangers should not seek out and destroy the crocodile that had tried to kill her," you can conclude that the author wants the reader to think that Plumwood
☐ a. has great respect for all animals.
☐ b. did not want the rangers to go to any trouble on her account.
☐ c. was not very knowledgeable about crocodiles.

4. In this article, "Finally, she came to a large swamp that separated her from the station, and her heart sank" means when she came to the swamp, she
☐ a. felt discouraged.
☐ b. fell to the ground.
☐ c. became ill.

---

_____ Number of correct answers

Record your personal assessment of your work on the Critical Thinking Chart on page 150.

CRITICAL THINKING

## Summarizing and Paraphrasing

Follow the directions provided for questions 1 and 3. Put an X in the box next to the correct answer for question 2.

1. Complete the following one-sentence summary of the article using the lettered phrases from the phrase bank below. Write the letters on the lines.

> **Phrase Bank:**
> a. Plumwood's canoeing in a national park in Australia
> b. Plumwood's analyzing the place of humans in nature
> c. Plumwood's encounter with the crocodile

The article "Death Roll in the River" begins with _____, goes on to describe _____, and ends with _____.

2. Choose the sentence that correctly restates the following sentence from the article: "Frantically, she tried again to climb to safety in the nearby tree."

☐ a. As hard as she tried, Plumwood could not reach the safety of the nearby tree.

☐ b. One more time, Plumwood desperately attempted to reach safety in the tree that was close to her.

☐ c. Plumwood kept trying to climb the tree, where she knew she would be safe.

3. Reread paragraph 3 in the article. Below, write a summary of the paragraph in no more than 25 words.

_____

_____

_____

_____

_____

> _____ Number of correct answers
>
> Record your personal assessment of your work on the Critical Thinking Chart on page 150.

## Critical Thinking

Put an X in the box next to the correct answer for questions 1, 4, and 5. Follow the directions provided for the other questions.

1. From what the article told about Val Plumwood, you can predict that she will

☐ a. write a children's story about a crocodile.

☐ b. always argue in favor of animal rights.

☐ c. never again travel alone in a canoe.

2. Choose from the letters below to correctly complete the following statement. Write the letters on the lines.

On the positive side, _____, but on the negative side, _____.

a. Plumwood survived a crocodile attack

b. it took months for Plumwood to recover from her injuries

c. Plumwood attempted to leap onto a tree branch to escape the crocodile

3. Reread paragraph 4. Then choose from the letters below to correctly complete the following statement. Write the letters on the lines.

According to paragraph 4, _____ because _____.

   a. a "death roll" is a short, intense burst of power

   b. crocodiles hold their prey under water

   c. victims of a crocodile attack drown

4. From the information in paragraph 3, you can conclude that Plumwood attempted to scare the animal before trying to reach the tree limb because Plumwood

   ☐ a. didn't believe the crocodile was dangerous.

   ☐ b. believed that any animal can be frightened away by a human.

   ☐ c. was angry that she would have to leave the canoe.

5. What did you have to do to answer question 3?

   ☐ a. find a cause (why something happened)

   ☐ b. find a contrast (how things are different)

   ☐ c. draw a conclusion (a sensible statement based on the text and your experience)

_____ Number of correct answers

Record your personal assessment of your work on the Critical Thinking Chart on page 150.

## Personal Response

A question I would like answered by Val Plumwood is

_____

_____

_____

_____

## Self-Assessment

Before reading this article, I already knew

_____

_____

_____

_____

_____

_____

_____

_____

_____

_____

# Compare and Contrast

Think about the articles you have read in Unit Three. Choose three articles that taught you the most about human behavior. Write the titles of the articles in the first column of the chart below. Use information you learned from the articles to fill in the empty boxes in the chart.

| Title | Did the survivor change as a result of the ordeal? How? | What lessons might be learned from the survivor's ordeal? | Could the person's survival be called heroic? Why or why not? |
|---|---|---|---|
| | | | |
| | | | |
| | | | |

Which survivor would you most like to meet? _____

Why? _____

_____

_____.

# Words-per-Minute Table

## Unit Three

**Directions** If you were timed while reading an article, refer to the Reading Time you recorded in the box at the end of the article. Use this words-per-minute table to determine your reading speed for that article. Then plot your reading speed on the graph on page 148.

| Lesson | 11 | 12 | 13 | 14 | 15 | |
|---|---|---|---|---|---|---|
| No. of Words | 1150 | 1142 | 1135 | 1140 | 1066 | |
| 1:30 | 767 | 761 | 757 | 760 | 711 | 90 |
| 1:40 | 690 | 685 | 681 | 684 | 640 | 100 |
| 1:50 | 627 | 623 | 619 | 622 | 581 | 110 |
| 2:00 | 575 | 571 | 568 | 570 | 533 | 120 |
| 2:10 | 531 | 527 | 524 | 526 | 492 | 130 |
| 2:20 | 493 | 489 | 486 | 489 | 457 | 140 |
| 2:30 | 460 | 457 | 454 | 456 | 426 | 150 |
| 2:40 | 431 | 428 | 426 | 428 | 400 | 160 |
| 2:50 | 406 | 403 | 401 | 402 | 376 | 170 |
| 3:00 | 383 | 381 | 378 | 380 | 355 | 180 |
| 3:10 | 363 | 361 | 358 | 360 | 337 | 190 |
| 3:20 | 345 | 343 | 341 | 342 | 320 | 200 |
| 3:30 | 329 | 326 | 324 | 326 | 305 | 210 |
| 3:40 | 314 | 311 | 310 | 311 | 291 | 220 |
| 3:50 | 300 | 298 | 296 | 297 | 278 | 230 |
| 4:00 | 288 | 286 | 284 | 285 | 267 | 240 |
| 4:10 | 276 | 274 | 272 | 274 | 256 | 250 |
| 4:20 | 265 | 264 | 262 | 263 | 246 | 260 |
| 4:30 | 256 | 254 | 252 | 253 | 237 | 270 |
| 4:40 | 246 | 245 | 243 | 244 | 228 | 280 |
| 4:50 | 238 | 236 | 235 | 236 | 221 | 290 |
| 5:00 | 230 | 228 | 227 | 228 | 213 | 300 |
| 5:10 | 223 | 221 | 220 | 221 | 206 | 310 |
| 5:20 | 216 | 214 | 213 | 214 | 200 | 320 |
| 5:30 | 209 | 208 | 206 | 207 | 194 | 330 |
| 5:40 | 203 | 202 | 200 | 201 | 188 | 340 |
| 5:50 | 197 | 196 | 195 | 195 | 183 | 350 |
| 6:00 | 192 | 190 | 189 | 190 | 178 | 360 |
| 6:10 | 186 | 185 | 184 | 185 | 173 | 370 |
| 6:20 | 182 | 180 | 179 | 180 | 168 | 380 |
| 6:30 | 177 | 176 | 175 | 175 | 164 | 390 |
| 6:40 | 173 | 171 | 170 | 171 | 160 | 400 |
| 6:50 | 168 | 167 | 166 | 167 | 156 | 410 |
| 7:00 | 164 | 163 | 162 | 163 | 152 | 420 |
| 7:10 | 160 | 159 | 158 | 159 | 149 | 430 |
| 7:20 | 157 | 156 | 155 | 155 | 145 | 440 |
| 7:30 | 153 | 152 | 151 | 152 | 142 | 450 |
| 7:40 | 150 | 149 | 148 | 149 | 139 | 460 |
| 7:50 | 147 | 146 | 145 | 146 | 136 | 470 |
| 8:00 | 144 | 143 | 142 | 143 | 133 | 480 |

Minutes and Seconds · Seconds

# Plotting Your Progress: Reading Speed

## Unit Three

**Directions** If you were timed while reading an article, write your words-per-minute rate for that article in the box under the number of the lesson. Then plot your reading speed on the graph by putting a small X on the line directly above the number of the lesson, across from the number of words per minute you read. As you mark your speed for each lesson, graph your progress by drawing a line to connect the Xs.

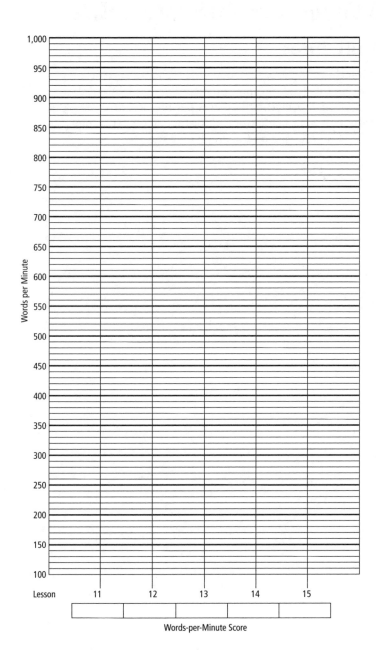

Words per Minute

Lesson   11   12   13   14   15

Words-per-Minute Score

# Plotting Your Progress: Reading Comprehension

## Unit Three

**Directions** Write your Reading Comprehension score for each lesson in the box under the number of the lesson. Then plot your score on the graph by putting a small X on the line directly above the number of the lesson and across from the score you earned. As you mark your score for each lesson, graph your progress by drawing a line to connect the Xs.

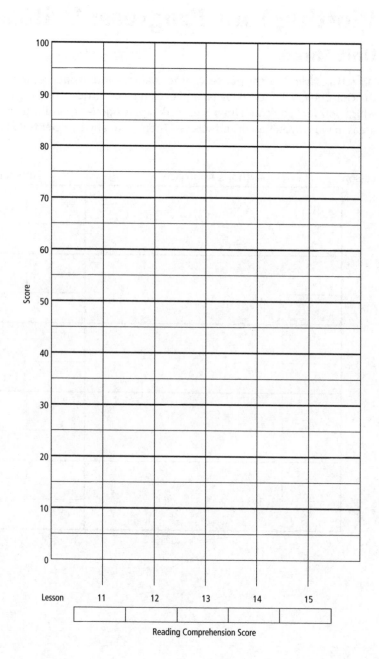

Score

Lesson    11    12    13    14    15

Reading Comprehension Score

# Plotting Your Progress: Critical Thinking

## Unit Three

**Directions** Work with your teacher to evaluate your responses to the Critical Thinking questions for each lesson. Then fill in the appropriate spaces in the chart below. For each lesson and each type of Critical Thinking question, do the following: Mark a minus sign (–) in the box to indicate areas in which you feel you could improve. Mark a plus sign (+) to indicate areas in which you feel you did well. Mark a minus-slash-plus sign (–/+) to indicate areas in which you had mixed success. Then write any comments you have about your performance, including ideas for improvement.

| Lesson | Author's Approach | Summarizing and Paraphrasing | Critical Thinking |
|---|---|---|---|
| 11 | | | |
| 12 | | | |
| 13 | | | |
| 14 | | | |
| 15 | | | |

# Image Credits